24 July 1911. Dawn.

'Leaving the stream, we now struggled
up the bank through dense jungle, and
in a few minutes reached the bottom
   of a very precipitous slope. For an
      hour and twenty minutes we had a
      hard climb...'

The Urubamba River
near Machu Picchu

24 July 1911.

'Richarte and Alvarez sent a small boy with me as a "guide". He urged us to climb up a steep hill over what seemed to be a flight of stone steps. We came to a great stairway of large granite blocks. Only a really small man could have passed along it in the time of the Incas!'

We would set up our camp just above this house, at the top of the drawing.

Early afternoon.

A young Indian boy from the Pampaconas Valley.

'Our guide led us along one of the widest terraces, and we made our way into an untouched forest beyond. Suddenly I found myself confronted with the walls of ruined houses built of the finest quality of Inca stone work. It was hard to see them for they were partly covered with trees and moss, the growth of centuries, but in the dense shadow, hiding in bamboo thickets and tangled vines, appeared here and there walls of white granite ashlars carefully cut and exquisitely fitted together. What a marvel!

September 1911. Start of the excavations.

'The clearance work has begun at Machu Picchu. Here, in the great temple, Lieutenant Sotomayor (on the right) directs the group of Indian workers.'

This must be more or less how the great Inca jars were carried.

Inca designs found on potsherds.

'Cave no. 9 is one of the biggest funerary caves. On its floor we found numerous skeletons...and fragments of marvellous pots which must have been placed there with the dead.'

'In cave no. 11, Dr Eaton, a specialist in osteology, is busy uncovering a human skeleton. The man on the right is a soldier generously "lent" by the Peruvian government to guarantee the security of the workers.'

We found this magnificent bronze knife depicting a fisherman.

These houses are rectangular, built of ashlars wedged with small irregular stones called 'Pachillas'.

This roofing technique is still used by present-day Quechuas.

'Here is one of the communal houses that made up the former city. There were several clans or families which each possessed from 6 to 16 houses.
The clusters of dwellings are all markedly different from each other. This one, for example, has very special stone masonry...'

'The houses probably had no furniture! Sometimes we found big flat stones which may have served as beds. In some corners there are even stone seats, like this one...'

Closing mechanism for doors, as far as we can gather from the surviving bolting system.

May 1912

'In one house we found a mortar, doubtless used for grinding maize or dried potatoes. Next to it was a big stone used as a pestle. The child placed it in the grinder exactly as though he was going to prepare a meal of maize for today...'

'Here is a group of sacred rocks surrounded by terraces. On the upper level, the stones reach extraordinary dimensions. Some are as big as a man. One wonders how the Incas could move them, without wheels or draught animals...I required a healthy dose of naivety...and a small army of workers to move these enormous rocks.

'Machu Picchu, in the midst of clearance operations. It is hard to imagine the final result...'

One of the 1912 expedition's first topographic surveys.

'Here, the clearance has performed wonders: the hill of the Intihuatana and the terraces to the west of the sacred plaza have at last emerged from the forest. On the left, vertiginous precipices, and

down below, the Urubamba foams and rumbles...

...The sacred city was well and truly impregnable!'

CONTENTS

THE INCAS
EMPIRE OF BLOOD AND GOLD
Carmen Bernand

THAMES AND HUDSON

In 1511 a rumour began to circulate among Spanish settlers in Panama that several days' journey to the south of the isthmus there stretched a vast kingdom, a fabulous country of untold riches. When this news reached the ears of Spanish explorer Vasco Núñez de Balboa, discoverer of the Pacific, it sounded like a challenge.

CHAPTER 1
IN SEARCH OF ELDORADO

By the 19th century the Incas had become a Romantic legend. Left: a wallpaper of 1826 showing the Incas worshipping the setting sun. Right: a 16th-century ship, comparable to those in which Pizarro and his companions sailed to Peru.

Exasperated by the greed of the foreigners who had settled in Panama under the leadership of Balboa, an Indian chief exhorted the intruders to go farther south in search of the gold after which they lusted so much. He claimed that a mysterious southern kingdom was so crammed with the precious metal that the people used it to make the most everyday objects. Besides the gold, the Indian chief also mentioned strange animals, which he drew, and which Núñez de Balboa took to be Arabian camels: they were llamas. But Balboa was the victim of a plot and perished by the headsman's axe without fulfilling the dream that these words had aroused in him.

Only a decade later, in 1522, the Spanish adventurer Pascual de Andagoya undertook the first expedition to the south. The voyage was a brief one, to be sure, but during the trip Andagoya heard, from the mouth of native merchants, a great deal of very detailed testimony about the existence of an immensely rich empire which stretched over hundreds of leagues to the south. This meeting between the Spaniard and the Andean merchants took place beside a river called the Biru, a name which would soon be used to denote the coveted country.

Attracted by Andagoya's reports, two conquistadors, already in their fifties, begin to dream of setting off themselves in search of Biru

Francisco Pizarro and Diego de Almagro lacked the means to undertake such an expedition, with its heavy expenditure and uncertain outcome. So they joined forces with a priest from Panama, Hernando de Luque, who supported them against the advice of the governor Pedro Arias de Avila. Two vessels were chartered and, in 1524, a first expedition set sail – but with no success. The boats sailed along a stifling and rainy coast, covered with mangroves and infested

Accounts by the conquistadors often failed to convey a very accurate image to European readers. These illustrations from the Netherlands and France depict the inhabitants of Peru as semi-naked savages; the warrior (below) wears a feather headdress, while the map (right) shows all sorts of fantastic creatures, including a llama – one of the many species hitherto unknown to European zoology.

with mosquitoes, which bore no resemblance to the Eldorado eulogized by Andagoya. Certainly, from time to time the Spaniards met a few natives who wore golden jewellery and told of a powerful southern kingdom. But having reached Punta Quemada on the Colombian coast, the horrified Spaniards discovered a cannibal tribe. This was too much. In the face of such hostility they gave up and returned to Panama.

Pizarro and his comrades on board their ship (left), a drawing made late in the 16th century by Felipe Guamán Poma de Ayala – a man with both Spanish and Inca blood in his veins, who left a unique record of Inca life. The natives themselves travelled in large sea-going rafts (below right).

The second expedition, in 1526–7, was more promising. While Pizarro stayed on land, the navigator Bartolomé Ruiz sailed on southwards. Off the present-day town of Tumaco, Ruiz saw a sailing vessel like a raft coming towards him. This was the first boat the Spaniards had encountered in these waters, since the Mexicans had never put to sea. On board the raft there were men and women, all dressed in superb, richly embroidered woollen fabrics that aroused the Europeans' admiration. Through interpreters from the isthmus, the Spaniards learned that the vessel came from a port called Tumbes, located at the modern frontier of Peru and Ecuador.

So, paradoxically, it is in the Pacific Ocean that the first meeting between the Spaniards and the inhabitants of the Andean Cordillera takes place

After explaining to the Spaniards that the fine wool of their clothes came from llamas, of which there were numerous herds in their country, the strangers confirmed that gold abounded there too. They mentioned the name of Huayna Capac, the Inca, sovereign of the whole country. Ruiz took a few of them on board with him to

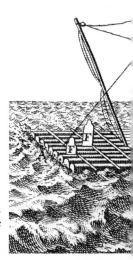

teach them Spanish and train them as interpreters; then
he rejoined Pizarro. Too few in number to attempt any
use of force in the Andean lands, the Spaniards sent
some of their group to seek reinforcements in Panama.
Pizarro and his men would await them on the Isla del
Gallo.

But when, after an exhausting journey, the ship did
come back, the conquistadors longed only to return to
Panama without even embarking on their adventure.
Only Pizarro remained fiercely determined. In front of
all his dispirited companions, he drew a dividing line on
the ground and declared:

'Comrades and
friends, on this side lie
poverty, hunger, effort,
torrential rains and
privation. On that side
lies pleasure. On this side,
we return to Panama and
poverty. On that side

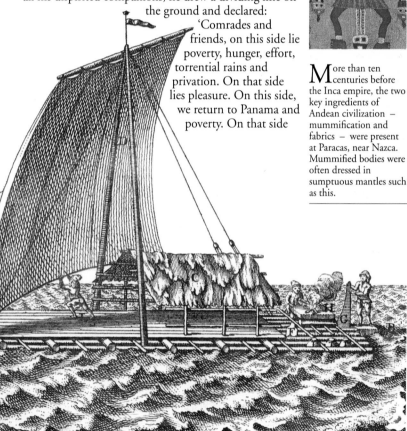

More than ten
centuries before
the Inca empire, the two
key ingredients of
Andean civilization –
mummification and
fabrics – were present
at Paracas, near Nazca.
Mummified bodies were
often dressed in
sumptuous mantles such
as this.

we go to Peru and become rich.' He was the first to cross this American Rubicon, followed by twelve faithful followers. History has immortalized these protagonists by the name of the 'Thirteen of the Isla del Gallo'.

The Spaniards did not, at first, succeed in penetrating the vast territory of the Andes, and had to content themselves with looking at Eldorado from the sea. Sailing along the present-day coast of Ecuador, they discovered, off the Río Guayas, the

It was in fighting the Moors of the Granada region that the Spanish learned how to counter guerrilla warfare. This experience, together with the superiority of their weaponry, was to prove advantageous in Peru. Above right: portrait of Pizarro by Vasquez Diaz Trujillo. Above left: Spanish sword and scabbard. Left: Spanish lancer and arquebusier.

imposing outline of Chimborazo. This volcano, 6400 m high, is visible from the sea in fine weather, despite the distance. As they progressed, the snowcapped mountains became clearer, forming an apparently impassable barrier between the foreigners and the Inca's country.

At Tumbes, a port with heavy sea-going traffic, the locals greeted the white men with kindness. Charmed by the beauty of the women, one of the Spaniards, Alonzo de Molina, decided to remain on land. The description that he later gave his comrades of the riches he had seen was so extraordinary that Pizarro decided to send another, more trustworthy messenger, Pedro de Candia. Dressed in armour that glinted in the sun, this man made a great impression on the natives. At their request he loaded his arquebus and fired, filling them with terror because the shot sounded like a clap of thunder, which they held in religious awe. Besides, the skin colour of the Spaniards startled the Andean people as much as that of their black slaves.

The Inca's army (below, in a coloured engraving of 1572) might have numbered more than 200,000 men, armed with bows, arrows, clubs, spears and slings. They wore padded jerkins that were more effective against arrows than against arquebus shots.

Laughter and exchanges of gifts: the conquest proceeds almost like a good-natured festival.... Indeed, the Spaniards are only a handful in number and can scarcely look threatening

Out of this smiling throng there stepped a person of distinction, whose serious air contrasted with the general relaxed attitude. He was an *orejón* ('big ears'), so-named by the Spaniards because the earlobes of the Inca's ambassadors were deformed by heavy ornaments. This dignitary, who represented the power of the state, inquired about the Spaniards' intentions. What had they come to seek in these countries so far from their own? When Pizarro spoke to him of the great emperor Charles V, the most powerful in the world, the dignitary said nothing. He accepted the gift of an axe of iron, a metal as yet unknown to the people of the Andes (or indeed to anyone in the Americas). Then, apparently discreetly, he dispatched a messenger to Quito, in modern-day

'On this side poverty, on that side riches' – Pizarro's famous moment of choice as seen by a 19th-century Romantic artist. Those who followed Pizarro were men of humble origin, founding their nobility not on blood inherited but on blood spilled.

Ecuador, where the Inca was campaigning, to inform the ruler of the arrival of these disturbing men.

Delighted by their welcome, the Spaniards sailed on as far as Chincha on the southern coast of present-day Peru; beyond here they came upon desert shores containing immense cemeteries. After this brief exploration they headed northwards once more. Passing Tumbes again, they took three young boys along to teach them Spanish; one of these was a certain Felipillo, who was to play a decisive role in the history of the conquest.

Coasting from port to port, the Spaniards gradually realized that in fact the Inca reigned over a mosaic of peoples who had only recently been subjugated. Indeed, when the conquistadors arrived the empire was little more than a century old. Its territory extended northwards to the province of Pasto (to the south of modern Colombia) and southwards to the Río Maule, in central Chile. Within this immense expanse there lived

At puberty, boys of royal lineage underwent a rite of passage called *huarachico*, during which their earlobes were perforated. They thus became warriors, and learned of the exploits of past dynasties by listening to the songs about them. The period of initiation lasted from October to December, and included mortifications and seclusion on the sacred mountain of Huanacauri. This tradition of the *orejónes* still exists today in other forms.

heterogeneous peoples, integrated in different ways into the whole.

How the Incas built up such a vast empire so quickly remains an enigma

The enigma is made all the more insoluble by the fact that the history of the successive dynasties and their victories often verges on legend. Although it has become apparent that the powerful families from which the Incas descended were originally established around Cuzco, in the heart of the Cordillera, it is extremely difficult to retrace precisely the chronological stages that led from the Cuzco confederation to the Inca empire.

According to the accounts gathered by the Europeans from actual members of the Inca Huascar's family, it was the Inca Pachacuti who, in the 15th century, built the formidable empire that was discovered by the dazzled Spaniards. The people of Cuzco referred to their empire as the 'Land of the Four

The Incas built citadels, *pucara*, throughout the empire. The most majestic fortress, that of Sacsahuaman, still overlooks the town of Cuzco. It is surrounded by a wall of stones that are so well fitted that a knife-blade cannot be inserted between them. It was defended, in Inca times, by three towers which communicated with the Inca's palace by underground passages.

Quarters', *Tahuantinsuyu*, a name that was both symbolic and administrative: the empire was arranged around Cuzco, the 'navel', in four great sectors orientated to the cardinal points. To the north stretched Chinchaysuyu; to the south Collasuyu, where the Lupaqa lords of Lake Titicaca lived; Cuntisuyu extended westwards; and, finally, Antisuyu opened on to the Amazonian piedmont, which the Incas never really managed to subjugate despite several attempts.

The Inca expansion may seem astounding, but one should not forget that it was in keeping with a long Andean tradition. At regular intervals through the centuries, brilliant all-conquering civilizations arose on the Cordillera. Thus, more than 500 years before Christ, the culture of Chavín emerged in the central Andes and extended its influence as far as the coast. Then, from the 10th century onward, both Tiwanaku, on the shore of Lake Titicaca, and Wari, in the region of Ayacucho, underwent considerable expansion.

T here was a succession of twelve Inca dynasties at Cuzco, the thirteenth Inca being Atahualpa. It is probable that the tales gathered by the Spaniards mingled myth and history. Nowadays there is agreement that the ninth sovereign, Pachacuti (top), should be considered the first historical Inca. His name means 'inversion of the world order'. It was he who rebuilt the town of Cuzco, constructed the roads, and promoted the cult of Viracocha. Above: Huascar Inca.

TU PA
YVPAN
INCAY

The number of Inca dynasties and their historical reality are a matter of debate. According to the best established theory, there were five Incas belonging to the Hurin dynasty and eight other sovereigns belonging to the Hanan dynasty, which was hierarchically superior. The emperor or Sapa Inca was himself the son of the Sun and was worshipped as such. No lord, no matter how powerful, could approach him without carrying a burden on his back, as a sign of humility. Paintings from the colonial period always represent the Inca kings with their emblems: the sceptre in the form of an axe, and the royal fringe or *mascapaicha*, which was red in colour. This 17th-century painting shows Topa Yupanqui (left) and the third Inca Lloque Yupanqui (right).

On the northern coast, around the 7th century, the Mochica developed an original culture as seen in its figurative ceramics. In the south – in those sepulchral regions that had impressed Pizarro's men so deeply – a people that archaeologists refer to by the generic term of Paracas produced America's finest woven textiles with which to cover their dead. In more recent times, the chiefdoms of Peru's northern coast had united to form the kingdom of Chimor, based at Chan Chan.

When compared with the splendour of the fabrics, ceramics and monuments produced by all these peoples, Inca art can sometimes look a little austere.

According to tradition, the first Incas emerged from the cave of Pacaritambo in the form of four men, the Ayar, and four women. A fanciful Italian engraving of 1820 shows Manco Capac and queen Mama Huaco accepting the submission of the natives.

The genius of the Incas lies not so much in the pursuit of traditions invented by others as in the political organization of a vast and ethnically heterogeneous country

For it is truly an art to govern many often hostile ethnic groups, an art that rests on three principles. First, the centralization of power in the city of Cuzco, a power personified by the Inca and which he seems to have shared with a close relative (although this political dualism is a matter of some debate); secondly, a bureaucratic system that administered the conquered provinces, with the *orejónes* as its mainstays; and finally, the obligatory use throughout the whole territory of the Quechua language, spoken by the Incas, to the detriment of all the local tongues.

However, the unification was not always accomplished without a hitch. The last lord of Chimor, in particular, courageously resisted the Incas – but in vain. And because the natives that Pizarro met at Tumbes belonged to that powerful kingdom, they resented Inca domination. The northern regions of the Ecuadorian Andes, which had been conquered with some difficulty at the beginning of the 16th century, also displayed a certain hostility to the central power.

In order to secure his dominion over these distant territories, the Inca resorted to a policy which has proved effective in many instances; it consists of moving entire populations so as to break up local solidarity. Hence families from Cuzco or other safe provinces were

transported thousands of kilometres and settled, for example, in the valleys near Quito or in those of Tucumán (Argentina).

These colonists, known as *mitimaes*, maintain ties with their families and their homeland, and thus form a nucleus loyal to the state in the midst of a foreign ethnic group

Conversely, groups belonging to regional chiefdoms were moved into areas that were culturally attached to the Cuzco authorities. Even so, rebellion continued to smoulder in many areas.

It was in the valleys of Nazca and Moche that original civilizations emerged; based on vast irrigation works, they served as a model for the Incas several centuries later. Thanks to the realism of its forms and depictions, Mochica pottery enables us to reconstruct certain aspects of this culture, in which shamanism, human sacrifice and ritual eroticism played an important role.

Thus, at the same time the Spaniards were sailing along the Pacific coasts, distressed at finding only unhealthy mangroves, a rebellion against the Inca's authority broke out in the equatorial region of Quito, which had only recently been conquered.

Huayna Capac, eleventh in the dynasty, went there in person and subdued the rebels with a cruelty that has stuck in local memory. At Otavalo in Ecuador, the corpses of the rebels were thrown into a lake and turned its waters red: since then it has been called Yawar Cocha, the 'lake of blood'.

This is very different from the peaceful picture of Inca expansion painted later by the Cuzco authorities and, incidentally, repeated in the Spanish accounts (for a long time our only source of information about the period, since the Incas did not use writing). Garcilaso de la Vega in particular, an 'Inca and Spanish' chronicler heavily influenced by Neoplatonic philosophy, used his writings to propagate widely the quite unrealistic image of great lords full of generosity and renowned for their wisdom.

Having pacified the territory, Huayna Capac reached Quito, the second city of the empire. There, gloomy portents announced that a catastrophe was imminent: an earthquake of unusual violence, terrifying visions and, finally, a messenger from Tumbes who warned of the arrival by sea of white men – all seemed to confirm the ill omens.

Misfortune arrives in the form of an unknown disease – smallpox – which spreads through the region taking dozens of lives, including that of the Inca

Huayna Capac died of smallpox without having met a single one of the foreigners who brought this terrible sickness to the empire.

His embalmed corpse was carried to Cuzco. A crisis began

In 1528, equipped with precise information and proof concerning the wealth of the mysterious country, Pizarro returned to Spain where Charles V granted him the governorship of a vast territory to be conquered. Pizarro also met Cortes who had returned in triumph from Mexico and who gave him precious advice about the tactics to use against the 'savages' of the New World.

over his succession, pitting Huascar, the legitimate son, against Atahualpa, the bastard. The former was named Inca at Cuzco, the latter was proclaimed sovereign at Quito.

While the Spaniards prepared themselves, certain they had found Eldorado, civil strife between Quito and Cuzco shook the region. Returning to Spain, Pizarro set about convincing the Crown that it should finance the conquest of Peru. It was a stroke of good fortune for him that he had to postpone his enterprise: five years later he was able to take advantage of the fratricidal war that was tearing the empire apart, so that he might himself destroy the dynasty of the Incas.

Huascar, depicted in this 17th-century painting, was the legitimate heir to the empire because his half-brother Atahualpa stemmed from a bastard branch. Pizarro tried to ally himself with Huascar, but Atahualpa's supporters took Huascar prisoner and assassinated him to prevent such a collaboration.

In 1532, Pizarro was back in Peru, this time for good. He had at his disposal 63 horsemen and 200 infantrymen – a paltry number, but he believed in his lucky stars. At Tumbes he found a town ravaged by war and pestilence, no longer the lively port he had known before.

CHAPTER 2

THE PASSION OF ATAHUALPA

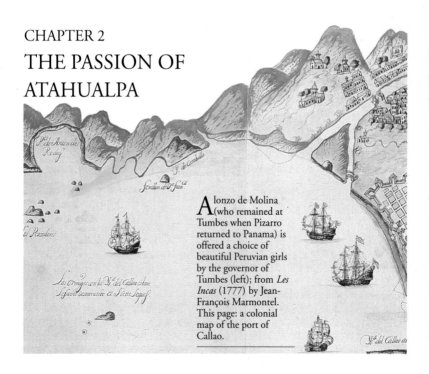

Alonzo de Molina (who remained at Tumbes when Pizarro returned to Panama) is offered a choice of beautiful Peruvian girls by the governor of Tumbes (left); from *Les Incas* (1777) by Jean-François Marmontel. This page: a colonial map of the port of Callao.

Fleeing these devastated regions the conquistadors headed into the mountains. They made for Cajamarca where they knew, from local scouts, that Atahualpa – one of the two warring brothers – was to be found. They followed a paved highway, similar to Roman roads, which scaled the steepest slopes by turning into a staircase. The section followed by Pizarro and his men formed part of a vast road system, the creation of which was attributed to the father of Huayna Capac, but which probably spanned several decades. Composed of two longitudinal axes (one following the coast, the other the crests of the Cordilleras) joined together by lateral roads, this remarkable network allowed effective communication between the provinces despite the formidable obstacles of the Andean mountain ranges. Messengers known as *chasquis* maintained interior connections, making all their journeys on foot. These runners apparently took over from each other every half a league; the service was so efficient that the Inca in the city of Cuzco could apparently eat fish that his *chasquis* brought him fresh from the seashore...

At Caxas, the conquistadors found a population exasperated by the cruelty of Atahualpa, and complaining of the heavy tribute imposed by the Incas. Not only did the central power levy a large part of everything they produced, but it also demanded that children be sacrificed to it every year.

Inca engineering astonished the Spaniards. The walls of Sacsahuaman (left) are an outstanding example of so-called 'cyclopean' masonry, its huge irregular stones fitted together with minute precision.

● Pizarro set out, with the horse and foot, marching along the sea coast, which was well peopled, and placing all the villages under the dominion of his Majesty; for their lords, with one accord, came out into the roads to receive the Governor, without making any opposition. The Governor, far from doing them any harm or showing any anger, received them all lovingly, and they were taught some things touching our holy Catholic Faith, by the monks who accompanied the expedition.●

Francisco de Xeres, *The Conquest of Peru,* 1534

Pizarro conquering Peru, from an engraving by Théodore de Bry (1602).

Chosen from the most beautiful children and, as a general rule, from powerful families, the future little victims are accorded every honour

Some made the journey to Cuzco, where they were received by the Inca with great pomp. On returning to their village, the children were entombed in caves or thrown down into gorges. Their death, which was meant to spare the Inca any suffering or illness, at the same time conferred great prestige on the families. It sometimes happened that the community itself decided to sacrifice

Inca law was harsh and clemency on the part of the rulers all the more gratefully received. In another 19th-century reconstruction, Mayta Capac pardons two malefactors.

one of its children to secure general prosperity. Although these practices were forbidden in the first years of Spanish colonization, they were to continue here and there until the start of the 20th century.

Far more common were the animal sacrifices which also had to follow certain rules: their coat had to be plain and their hair silky, for example. According to some chroniclers, in the city of Cuzco they sometimes killed more than 10,000 llamas in the course of a single ceremony, by throwing them on to a fire. This figure, though probably an exaggeration, nevertheless gives some indication of the scale of the rite.

At the entry of Caxas the Spaniards noticed three corpses hanging by the feet. When they asked the reason for this punishment, they were told that these men had dared enter the house of the *aclla*, the women vowed to the Inca's service. Chosen from the most beautiful girls of each ethnic group, separated from the community of their birth and cloistered for life, they could neither marry nor have sexual relations without the sovereign's permission. Anyone who dared to cross the threshold of their residence was condemned to death, and their families disgraced. In the house reserved for them, the *aclla* – who were similar to the vestals – devoted themselves to weaving the Inca's clothes. Indeed weaving was one of the key elements of Inca civilization, and Pizarro and his men, having already understood that all trade depended on it, eagerly offered shirts from Castile to the inhabitants of Caxas.

Amazed by the quality of the Andean fabrics, the Spaniards very quickly learned to distinguish the *ahuasca*, worn by the common people, from the precious *cumbi*, the privilege of the elite, who shunned alpaca and llama wool in favour of the soft fleece of the vicuña.

In the region of Lake Titicaca, the people used to sacrifice a black llama, the *urcu*, before setting off to war (left); drawing by Guamán Poma de Ayala.

Chosen from each community for their beauty, the *aclla* were given to the Inca as a sign of allegiance. He could then redistribute these women to the nobles as a reward for their services.

The sin of Cora the priestess

In Jean-François Marmontel's novel, *Les Incas* (1777), Alonzo de Molina falls in love with Cora, a priestess of the Sun, and she with him. By a fortunate chance he is able to rescue her from her convent during a volcanic eruption. They wander in the fields and enjoy a brief idyll of happiness before Cora, in fear, returns to the Temple. Although fictitious, it does reflect a proven historical reality. The virgins of the Sun renounced normal relationships: they prepared food and drink for their 'husband', the Sun. Consecrated at the age of twelve in a cycle of ceremonies, they then underwent a kind of noviciate that lasted three years, at the end of which the high priest invited them to make a definitive choice between marriage and consecration to the Sun as an *aclla*.

The Inca's law

If a woman consecrated to the Sun betrayed her vows by falling in love with a mortal and losing her virginity, she was buried alive and her lover was hanged. The Inca also killed the man's wife, children and entire family, as well as every member of his community (*ayllu*) and their animals. The houses of his village were razed, and the earth sprinkled with salt so that nothing would grow and this accursed place would serve as a warning to everyone. (Cora and her family almost meet this fate. But in Marmontel's novel Alonzo steps forward, takes the blame upon himself and, with the characteristic optimism of the Enlightenment, persuades the Inca to abolish the priestesses' vow of celibacy.) Isabel Yarucpalla, one of Atahualpa's wives, was given to the conquistador Juan Lobato de Sosa, one of the founders of Quito. She adopted the Spanish way of life and even thwarted a plot by the officials of Quito to massacre the Spanish and join the rebellion of the Inca Manco.

The conquistadors soon understand that in Andean societies weaving has a far more important function than the strictly utilitarian

The Inca used *cumbi* to demonstrate his generosity when he appointed his associates: if a lord swore him allegiance, the ruler rewarded the noble by offering him some *cumbi*, thus securing his loyalty. One chronicler reports that when the conflict over the succession broke out, Atahualpa sent Huascar some fabrics of extreme beauty. The latter, furious, threw them on the fire, crying: 'Does he think that we don't have equally beautiful ones here, or is he just trying to hide his treason with this gift?'

Pizarro, who was just beginning to learn about Andean customs, had not yet grasped the significance of these fabrics; but a few years later his compatriots had the designs on them interpreted by informants who still remembered their meaning, and began to speculate that they constituted a form of writing. According to some testimony, the Incas were able to record the history of the dynasties on the embroideries (*quellca*). Indeed the word *quellca* was used in the colonial period to mean writing. The finest *quellca* were sent, in 1570, to Philip II of Spain to decorate the walls of the Escorial. Unfortunately, all trace of these cloths has been lost, and the mystery of their meaning remains unsolved.

Textile workshops (such as those in this 17th-century drawing) were founded by the Spaniards on the basis of the Incas' ancestral knowledge of weaving. Soon after the conquest, they were to become true capitalist enterprises with a native workforce. The products that were manufactured were made for local markets, which enabled them to avoid the taxes levied on European merchandise. Despite the deplorable working conditions, the workshops were extremely successful, especially in the northern Andes.

Trophy-heads such as those on these Paracas textiles (left) are a common motif in the iconography of the coastal civilizations, and recall the human head-hunting practised by the Amazonian populations. The Incas did not practise decapitation. Instead, defeated enemies were massacred, the chiefs flayed, and their stretched skin used as a membrane for drums.

A wool and braid ornament (above), in the form of a figure.

Leaving Caxas, Pizarro set out across frozen heathlands. In places the altitude reached 4000 m, the cold was intense, and the horses 'caught cold'. The Spaniards encountered pyramidal stone fortresses and storehouses filled with fabrics and food, intended to meet the armies' needs for several weeks. They stopped in the *tambos*, a kind of circular inn kept by old men. Crossing the rivers was another cause for astonishment: whereas in the plains crossings were made by raft, the mountain torrents were overhung with rope bridges or suspended baskets operated from the banks by cables. All these crossing points were supervised, and nobody could carry a load over them without paying a toll.

There were several kinds of bridge: slabs resting on stone pillars called *rumichacas*; simple tree trunks; or suspension bridges made from lianas and plaited agave fibres – like that at Penipé (left) or the one that still hangs over the Apurimac River. Alternatively, the traveller could use an *oroya*, a kind of basket in which he or she could slide along a cable (far left). A *Chaca Suyuyoc*, or 'governor of the royal bridges', was in charge of all these civil engineering works.

The use of the road network is subject to very strict controls, which nobody can avoid on pain of death

Even before reaching Cajamarca, therefore, the Spaniards learned that they were dealing with a 'highly controlled culture' very different from the confusion that reigned in the northern chiefdoms. Arriving in the town where Atahualpa had established his headquarters, the conquistadors soon realized that their little band's only resource against this powerfully organized civilization was cunning. It did not take long for the fear inspired by the horses and the arquebuses to die down, nor for the Incas to become aware that the white men were vulnerable. Atahualpa certainly intended to exploit the foreigners, or at least to use them against Huascar. Thus, tension began to mount beneath the sun of Cajamarca.

The fortress of Ingapirca, famous for its circular shape, was built at the time of the conquest of the region of the Cañari, a people who lived to the south of present-day Ecuador.

This town impressed the Spaniards even more than Caxas. Its central square, bigger than the largest square in Spain, was bordered by beautifully proportioned buildings of fitted stone, whose construction displayed a remarkable architectural technique. One superb building devoted to the cult of the Sun stood at the town entrance. A messenger explained to the strangers that Atahualpa was fasting. Both sides awaited the meeting. Envoys were exchanged. Each side watched the other. Finally, Pizarro sent his brother Hernando to the emperor.

The conquistador finds the Inca seated on a low chair, surrounded by numerous dignitaries and a few of his women, including his own sister

The sovereign, whom Hernando reckoned to be about thirty years old, was dressed in the most delicate fabrics, and crowned with the royal insignia – a woollen braid wound five times around the head, from which there hung a fringe of wool interwoven with gold, covering part of his forehead. Each of his earlobes was encrusted with a gold disc. Atahualpa's face was hidden by a very fine fabric: he was the son of the Sun, and his person was too powerful to be seen by human eye. But the Spaniards demanded that the sovereign remove the veil, which he did, though without bestowing a single glance on them. Then he exhorted them to return all the woven fabrics they had stolen en route. After this somewhat frosty conversation, Atahualpa nevertheless agreed to meet Pizarro on the square of Cajamarca. Next he offered the Spaniards some maize beer in large

An 18th-century print of the Inca and his wife (below left). Right: Inca princes and a princess; the first is in Spanish costume, the other two in traditional dress.

TEMPLE DU SOLEIL.

The solar cult was imposed throughout the empire, adding to the many local cults. The most important event in the religious calendar was the festival of the Sun or Inti Rami, celebrated at the June solstice. On this occasion, the lords would come to Cuzco to deliver tribute to the Inca who, in return, gave them women and other prestige goods. The Incas also went to the temple of Vilcañota (one of the most prestigious in the empire along with that of Pachacamac), and their pilgrimage relived the mythical journey of the first Inca, Manco, and his wife, Mama Huaco. Here, children from every province were sacrificed to the Sun.

golden vases. The conquistadors refused at first. But they had to give way at Atahualpa's threatening insistence. It was the custom: in order to open negotiations, the more powerful party offered a drink, which could not be refused without causing offence.

The decisive meeting between the two sides took place the following day. Pizarro ordered his men to hide, and be ready to intervene if he called out the name of Saint James. The appearance of the Inca was an extraordinary spectacle: he arrived, carried in a litter lavishly decorated with parrot feathers, and surrounded by bodyguards covered in sheets of gold and dressed in the richest costumes. The imperial procession was preceded by a troop of youngsters who swept the ground with meticulous care. A colourfully dressed crowd escorted it, to the sound of conch shells and flutes.

Atahualpa's meeting with Pizarro in the square of Cajamarca was the great turning-point of South American history. This engraving, made soon after the event, shows him borne on a litter by his lords (below).

ATHABALIBA

The title of Inca was hereditary but, among his descendants, the sovereign would choose the son who was best suited to succeed him. It seems that the Inca was seconded by a close relative, who is sometimes mentioned as a military chief. Royal incest – the model for which was the mythical couple of Manco and Mama Huaco – preserved the dynasty's endogamous reproduction, while polygamy enabled the sovereign to forge solid alliances with the regional *caciques.* It is said that Atahualpa (left) had more than 5000 concubines.

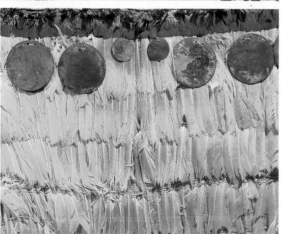

Among the goods that the Incas levied from the tribes of the Amazonian piedmont, gold and feathers of rare birds – especially of macaws living in the Amazonian forest – were considered the most precious. This Chancay textile uses both feathers and gold.

Under their brightly coloured clothes, the Cajamarcans hide slings and clubs...

From 25 to 50 years of age, a man was *aucacamayoc*, an adult in every sense – warrior (left), labourer, miner. He was in the service of the princes and the principal nobles.

In less than an hour the destiny of the empire was completely overturned. On Pizarro's orders, Vicente de Valverde, a Dominican priest, advanced towards the Inca brandishing a cross in one hand and a Bible or breviary in the other: 'I have come to teach you the words of God.' Atahualpa seized the book, put it to his ear, and threw it violently to the ground: no sound had come out of the object, whereas the ancestors and the sacred places spoke to men through their priests! This impious gesture unleashed Pizarro's anger; he grabbed the arm of the son of the Sun, whom nobody was supposed to touch, and tried to throw him down from the litter. A terrible confusion followed, punctuated by the neighing of horses and arquebus shots. When calm was restored, the square was strewn with bodies. There remained only terrorized locals and a dishonoured Emperor, his clothes torn and his hands tied.

Atahualpa tried to save his head by proposing to Pizarro that he would fill a room of his dwelling with all the treasures of his kingdom. This would be the price of his ransom. From the coast, the mountains, from the four corners of the land there flowed numerous loads of precious objects. Atahualpa, imprisoned, waited and struck up a friendship with Hernando, Pizarro's brother. Together they played interminable games of dice. The Inca, in his gilded prison, was authorized to keep his women and his clothes, such as the magnificent cape of bat hair that his guards so admired. The ransom accumulated, and Pizarro reserved one fifth for the king of Spain. The chronicler Francisco López de Gómara reported that he appropriated for himself the big plate of gold that the Inca had in his litter.

Never had soldiers become so rich, nor so quickly. And never were such fortunes squandered so rapidly, mostly at the throw of a dice.

Atahualpa promises to fill the room with gold as ransom for his life (left). The golden vases and objects were melted into ingots, and today very little Inca gold survives (above: a Chimú knife with gold handle). It has been calculated that there were more than 5720 kg of gold and more than 11,000 kg of silver. Silver was so abundant that the Spaniards used it to shoe their horses. Pizarro, having set apart the king's share of the booty and his own, shared out the rest among his men.

While Pizarro brings Cajamarca to its knees, some generals faithful to Atahualpa assassinate Huascar, suspecting him of collaborating with the Spaniards, for whom reinforcements are now arriving. The Inca empire collapses

It was while Hernando, Atahualpa's only friend, was absent that the drama came to its climax. Alarming news reached Pizarro from Quito: breaking the truce established by the Inca's capture, one of his generals was threatening to come to Cajamarca to liberate his lord. Did Pizarro fear a rebellion, or did he use these rumours as a pretext to break his promise? The fact remains that he accused Atahualpa of high treason and condemned him to die at the stake, like an infidel. One cannot

Atahualpa's funeral – a 19th-century painting. Before surrendering to the executioner, Atahualpa begged Pizarro to take care of his children. His corpse remained on show in the square throughout the night and, the following day, it was carried into the church of San Francisco. It is said that his loyal supporters secretly exhumed the body and transported it to Quito.

imagine a crueller sentence: the Incas had an absolute terror of cremation because it caused the body to disappear. So Atahualpa agreed to convert to Catholicism on condition that he have his head cut off instead. He swore that, if decapitated, he would return one day to avenge his people. Even today, in the mountains of Peru, myths circulate that promise the impending return of Inkarri, a kind of new Messiah whose head has sprouted beneath the earth.

On the day of Atahualpa's execution, the sky became dark. Some of his wives and his sister hanged themselves, to accompany him and serve him in the afterlife, a very widespread custom in the northern Andes on the death of a great lord. Pizarro hastened to enthrone one of Atahualpa's younger brothers as Inca, a weak and

For the Romantic writers and artists of the 19th century, the Inca civilization became a sort of Golden Age, imagined as a society of peace and harmony that was far from the truth. Above: a section of panoramic wallpaper of 1826.

therefore easily manipulable character. But this child died some time afterwards, having been poisoned. At Pizarro's wish once again, another of the Inca's brothers, Manco, took his place and became sovereign.

Pedro, Pizarro's cousin, gives an entirely different version of Atahualpa's end: according to him, the emperor's death was plotted by Felipillo, the young interpreter from Tumbes whom the Spaniards took along during their first coastal voyage. Felipillo had good reason to hate the Inca, for he was a vassal of the lord of Chimor, who had been forced to capitulate to Atahualpa's predecessor, Huayna Capac. Moreover, during Atahualpa's captivity, the boy had fallen in love with one of the Inca's wives and conceived the idea of betraying him by producing a deliberately false translation of some crucial information, which then cost the fallen emperor his life.

Topa Amaru (right), the last Inca, was defeated and executed in 1572, and his head displayed on the end of a pike. He was renowned for his beauty. According to legend, the head became more beautiful every day, and his supporters came by night to worship it in secret. In order to put an end to this cult, the viceroy had it buried. Spanish law and order, embodied in Toledo's government, were henceforth to act ruthlessly.

Atahualpa's death seals the fate of the empire of the Four Quarters. The Spaniards enter the city of Cuzco and pillage the temple of the Sun

But the colonial administration had to endure some troubled years at the start. There were problems on two fronts. On the one hand, the Spaniards began to quarrel among themselves, forming two factions; one was led by Pizarro, the other by his erstwhile companion, Almagro. Both were to perish. On the other hand, the natives still refused to submit. After being cruelly humiliated by the Spaniards, the puppet Inca, Manco, fled with his army to the fortress of Vitcos, from where he organized the resistance.

His sons Titu Cusi and Topa Amaru would continue the struggle until 1572, when the latter was captured by the Spaniards and beheaded, just as his uncle Atahualpa had been forty years earlier. For two hundred years, Spanish law was to reign supreme in the Cordilleras.

The main Spanish leaders died feuding among themselves. Pizarro was assassinated in his palace in Lima on 26 July 1541.

D.ⁿ Felipe Tupa A...
...ın Ynga Vltimo de los Ir...
...eniltes de el Peru fue Casado...
...sus Ritos Jentilicos Conuirtiose al...
...a Real Estirpe, y Ynfiels Eclese...
...ª Juana Quispe sie a de la q.ᵉ tous...
...Calificado hasta oy Nueve hijos le...
...aso desta vida al ielcina en el año...
...Reciviendo Igracia de el Bautismo...
...se Degolado en Publico Cadalso...
...xesistentie ino SD. Fran.ᶜ Toledo...
...estos R.ˢ con desaprovencion dela...
...S.ᵒ Felipe 2.ᵒ y fue Sepultado en la...
...Corte de N.P.S. Domingo del Cuzco...
...gdel senhriad a a su Real Pavilia

54

TRAVAXOS
PAPAALLAIMITAPA

cha junio haucaycusqui quilla

labrador
pachaca

Once the empire was overthrown, the conquistadors established the *encomienda*, an institution that was to prove catastrophic for the country's social and economic order, and which began by unleashing bloody conflicts between the colonists and the Spanish Crown.

CHAPTER 3

EVERYDAY LIFE AND WORK

Under Spanish rule, the natives were obliged to work harder than before for less reward (left). Their agricultural methods are depicted here by Guamán Poma de Ayala. Right: fighting between the Spanish factions.

As a reward for their efforts, the conquistadors were granted the right to levy tribute from the Andean peoples. In return, they undertook to protect and evangelize the native people placed under their authority. This was known as the *encomienda* system; it was similar to feudal commanderies, and founded on ties of dependence rather than actual ownership of a domain. But the Spanish king soon began to disapprove of the powerful factions forming in the Americas, for he was able to exert very little control over them. So, under the pretext of putting an end to the abuses being committed there (of which he kept himself well informed), he decided to change the system and suppressed the perpetuity of the privilege. This measure sparked off a crisis. The conquistadors refused to yield, and rebelled against the representatives of the Crown.

It was only after some murderous struggles that the royal authority was finally asserted. It was decreed that the *encomiendas* would remain in the conquerors' hands until the second generation, and then revert to their natural owner, the king. These arrangements were not always respected, however, and some *encomiendas* endured until the 18th century. The *encomenderos* used their privileges to increase their political influence and, in particular, to misappropriate native labour to their own ends. The locals tirelessly denounced these machinations before the courts: this may appear strange, but all the natives of the region were vassals of the king of Spain and were, as such, protected by specific legislation.

The oppression of the native peoples by the Spanish privileged class, which began with the conquest, was to last for three hundred years. Here, in an engraving of 1532, they are forced to carry away plunder for their Spanish masters.

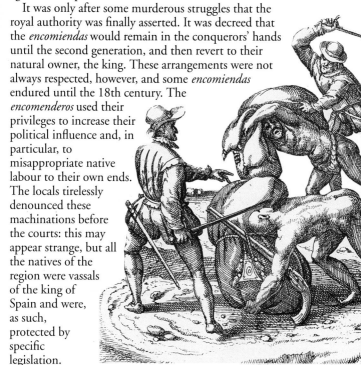

Forty years after the events in Cajamarca, the natives' situation has deteriorated dramatically in every way

Wars and epidemics caused a major demographic collapse, and the *encomienda* broke up the organization of the peasant communities. Many fled to escape the forced labour imposed on them by the Spaniards, and sought refuge in the towns.

In order to put an end to the haemorrhage of the workforce that was undermining the economic foundations of the colonial system, the viceroy Francisco de Toledo conceived extensive administrative reforms, based on territorial reorganization: in the accessible areas, villages were created and the peasantry redistributed among them.

Philip II developed the politics of centralization that had been established by his predecessor, Charles V. King Charles created the viceroyship of Lima in 1543. An alter ego of the monarch, the viceroy was governor, chief of the armies and president of the courts of justice. Around him was organized a court which reproduced, on a more modest scale, the pomp of that in Spain. His power was based on a bureaucratic system that divided up the territory. The important administrative posts were occupied by the viceroy's relatives, since nepotism and corruption were an inherent part of the colonial system.

These agglomerations were all laid out on a checkerboard plan, arranged around a central square bordered by the official buildings and the church. Such *reducciones*, which brought together members of different ethnic groups (and were used, where necessary, to disperse the members of a single ethnic group), would gradually turn into parishes, under the protection of a patron saint.

From the second half of the 16th century onwards, Spanish officials travelled through the Cordilleras compiling a census of inhabitants and resources. Their task was easy, since the natives had always kept extremely precise records of agriculture, demography and tribute. So the foreigners merely had to obtain from the mouths of the local dignitaries – the *quipucamayoc* ('keepers of the *quipu*') – the information that the latter had recorded by means of knotted strings. Known as *quipu*, the strings constituted an information-storage system which denoted and enumerated different classes of people, plants or objects. Although the language of these *quipu* has not been fully deciphered, we know that they also recorded non-quantitative information, such as songs or dynastic tales; but the code has been lost.

The village of Palca (top), with a traditional-style church surrounded by a wall. Above: porters carrying travellers on their backs.

Inca society is based on agriculture, and the Inca himself ritually takes part in the great labour of sowing and harvesting

It was the sovereign who inaugurated the seasonal cycle of maize, a cycle punctuated by ceremonies aimed at increasing the fecundity of both humans and plants. The simplicity of the toolkit available to the Inca people is astounding when one considers the enormous labour and management demanded by a territory that was so poorly adapted to agricultural exploitation. Sparse and stony soils, very steep slopes, difficult irrigation: the

Knotted strings, or *quipu,* continued to be used as accounting devices after the conquest. The size of the knots and the colours used made it possible to record quantities with extreme precision (measures of coca, maize or other agricultural products, numbers of tributaries, thefts of which the indigenous populations had been the victims during the conquistadors' campaigns, debts that the *encomenderos* had contracted with them). There were even 'historical' *quipu* which recorded the most outstanding episodes of the Inca dynasties. The drawing is by Poma de Ayala.

Incas succeeded in overcoming all these handicaps by building terraces and canals that are still in use today. In order to bring water to arid land, they altered the course of rivers and bored through rock which constituted an amazing technical feat considering they lacked iron tools. In fact, these techniques were in use before the Inca empire was established, but the state organization of the sovereigns of Cuzco made it possible to work on a much grander scale than had been hitherto possible. The most important agricultural tool used was a wooden spade, known as the *taclla*. They did not know the plough and, like draught oxen, the ard would never completely replace the old methods, at least not in the poorest areas.

Agriculture was mostly based on maize, coca and tubers (for instance, potatoes, quinoa and oca). Potatoes grow well at high altitudes, even above 4000 m, and, without this staple, the plateaux could never have been populated by humans. In the region of Lake Titicaca, where the potato originated, dozens of varieties have been recorded. Thanks to special climatic conditions, the Andean people managed to preserve potatoes for the lean months of the year: the sharp variation beween the nightly frosts and the tropical sun effected a process of dehydration which turned the potatoes into *chuño*. This is still the staple food of many of the populations living in the high plateaux.

The sacred valley of the Incas follows the middle section of the Urubamba, a few kilometres from Cuzco. At Pisac (left), the stepped terraces traversed the slopes for several hundred metres and produced the finest maize in the empire, especially destined for the lords' rituals. The whole valley belonged to the Inca and the royal lineages. Below: a peasant digging the ground with the peculiarly shaped Peruvian spade.

Maize, which grows in the relatively warm valleys, is more than a mere food: endowed with ritual and symbolic value, it is offered to the ancestors and to the divinities of the earth and the cosmos

According to Inca mythology, the first *Coya*, Mama Huaco (sister and wife of the Inca), was responsible for the origin of maize: she is said to have brought corn cobs out of the cave of Pacaritambo, the legendary place from which the founding Incas also emerged. For this reason, maize was also called 'cave seeds'. The myth survives in southern Ecuador, where some still believe that Mamahuaca, mistress of the mountains and announcer of harvests, hides in a cave with a basket of golden corn ears.

Coca had been cultivated for a very long time in the warm and rainy regions. During the reign of the Incas, only members of the elite had the right to chew it, a privilege accorded to the common people in exceptional circumstances alone. The abolition of such restrictions at the end of the empire led to extensive consumption of the plant, because coca could keep both hunger and fatigue at bay. Traffic in the crop was soon established, and this very quickly made a fortune for the Spaniards. Like maize, coca also had a sacred nature: it was used as an offering and as an instrument of divination – sorcerers and healers read the future in the patterns made by the leaves when they were thrown on the ground at random.

Apart from these crops, the Incas also raised herds of

Chewing dried coca leaves was a practice so widespread among all adults, men and women, that they always carried a little bag of woven wool (below) to hold the leaves.

Ancient Peruvian farming was geared to produce both food and luxury goods. In this 17th-century watercolour (right) the most prominent features are macaws, used to make feather garments, and maize, the staple food. Left: a llama and a vicuña, both kept for their beautiful wool.

le Lama e la Vigogne.

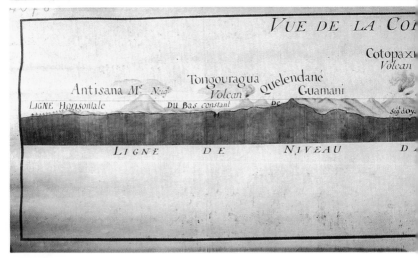

camelids, especially around Lake Titicaca. The principal value of these animals was their precious wool. Even when they were used as beasts of burden, they carried only light loads: heavier weights were transported on the backs of human porters. As for the hunts organized by the Inca, their function was ritual rather than utilitarian or recreational.

Before the Spanish arrived, the land was exploited collectively: families helped each other according to very strict rules of reciprocity, and at sowing and harvest time big gatherings were held during which maize beer (nowadays known as *chicha*) flowed like water. The Spaniards very quickly grew to be wary of these libations, which sparked off quarrels and engendered a strong sense of solidarity among the native populations.

In the Cordilleras, high altitudes and tropical or equatorial latitudes create a series of different geographical zones, one above the other

In Ecuador, for example, a very dense forest covers the slopes between 2800 and 3000 m. In ancient Peru and Bolivia, the zone above 3000 m was considered to be the most appropriate zone for permanent habitation; it was here that the Incas built their villages, close to the maize

The volcanoes of the northern Cordillera were considered in Inca society to be the abode of supernatural beings who unleashed lightning and thunder. They formed couples and could take on human shape. The lakes that formed in the craters were also inhabited by these divinities, to whom the peasants brought offerings of plants or human beings.

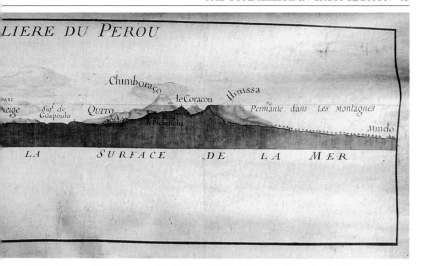

fields. Above 4000 m stretched the cold heathlands of the *puna*, which was devoted to pasture and the cultivation of tubers. Finally, below 2000 m, the Incas tended their coca and cotton plantations.

The ideal, for Andean communities, was to be able to exploit all three ecological levels, for in this way they could have access to all the necessary resources. Since these zones were sometimes quite a distance from each other, the communities would send families of colonists – *mitimaes* – to the lowlands and highlands to spend a few months cultivating there. The term *mitimaes* also referred to any displaced population, as well as the military garrisons installed by the Inca in annexed territories.

The originality of this system of land use lay not only in the permanent establishment of agricultural colonies detached from the nucleus of the home-village, but also in the exploitation of a single zone by several different ethnic groups, stemming from several centres. This concept of territory contrasts markedly with that of the Europeans, for whom an agricultural domain is always in a single block. It also involves a different way

The flowers and fruits of the New World fascinated European botanists, and were only slowly catalogued. This detail comes from a book published in 1802.

of appropriating the earth's products, and shows furthermore that ethnic barriers do not constitute an impediment to the collective utilization of a single zone.

In Peru, as across the whole of the Americas, the conquest is characterized by the exchange of plants, animals and techniques of domestication

The Spaniards studied native plants and began to incorporate them in their daily diet, as well as using

them for medicinal purposes. At the same time, the introduction of potatoes to Europe enabled the peasants there to overcome famine. Conversely, the domestic animals imported by the conquerors – cows, horses, mules, pigs, chickens, goats and sheep – transformed the ecological balance, dietary practices, and social relationships in general, of the Andean world. The horse, forbidden to the common people, could only be ridden by descendants of the elites, and thus became a symbol of social superiority; sheep displaced llamas; and pigs and cattle damaged the cereal fields, despite the fact that the Spaniards banned pastures on the edge of community lands.

Like all great civilizations, Inca Peru was based primarily on the tribute paid by the peasantry. The *quipucamayoc* took care of the accounts, and officials, generally given the name of 'caciques', kept a watchful eye on the work being done. The *cacique*, placed at the

These big sea conches or *mullu* were used as trumpets, their solemn sound marking the rhythms of communal work and of every ceremony. They had great value, and played a role in commercial transactions, though were not a form of money. Being precious objects, they also served as offerings.

Every four years, a vicuña and deer hunt took place on the high plateaux, depicted in this 17th-century illustration. The Inca himself took an active part in these hunts, which mobilized thousands of people.

head of a community comprising a group of domestic units (*ayllu*), redistributed the land every year according to the number of active people in each household. These ancient customs underwent a preliminary reorganization in Inca times, when the land at the disposal of each *ayllu* was divided into three unequal parts: the biggest was given to the community to farm, while the other two were consecrated to the cult of the Sun and the state respectively. The communities also paid a tribute of textiles (which were stockpiled in the state depots), and they were periodically subject to a labour tax,

The Spaniards imported into Peru huge numbers of domestic animals previously unknown there, such as horses, donkeys, cows, oxen, mules, dogs, sheep, goats, rabbits and pigs. These animals proliferated with great speed and some, for instance rabbits and pigs, became wild again and provided the indigenous communities with a new subsistence activity: hunting. The techniques of hunting large game were more or less the same in all the Andean regions: the men formed a vast circle which took in the whole terrain. By moving towards its centre they surrounded the animals, which were felled with pikes and clubs. The meat was dried and thus preserved for several months.

known as *mit'a* service, levied during the construction of all collective works, including highways, monuments and irrigation canals.

For administrative purposes, the different provinces comprising the empire of the Four Quarters were divided into groups of 10, 50, 100 or 1000 tributaries, which fitted into each other rather like Russian dolls; they were made up of all able-bodied men from 18 to 50 years of age.

The collectivization of work gives considerable advantage to the heads of large families

Four *waranga*, each comprising a group of 1000 tributaries, constituted an important economic unit, and was presided over by a delegate from the city of Cuzco; the latter was quite frequently a member of the imperial family. The principle of division into four went beyond the framework of simple quantification, for it expressed a very subtle symbolic conception of space.

Cut into the hardest granite, the canals built by the Incas constitute one of that civilization's technical miracles.

The Incas were anxious to control quite rigorously the social categories which determined who was liable to pay tribute. Marriage, the primary condition for becoming a fully fledged tributary, was a matter of state, and could only be contracted with the consent of the sovereign or his representative. A man of good position could enjoy several women (one of whom was considered the principal wife, 'given by the Inca'), and these would share a communal residence. Such polygamy provided the tributary both with a workforce for the production of

fabrics and, even more importantly, with numerous progeny.

So, on their arrival, the Spaniards find an elaborate system of tribute and a work-discipline which they could exploit shamelessly

It is noteworthy that the Quechua language has more than four hundred expressions for describing human activities. This valorization of effort explains the ease with which the Inca populations submitted to the new rules for paying tribute, even if they all complained to the investigators of the viceroy Toledo about the increased burden of labour that weighed them down and threatened their own crops.

In 1545 the Spaniards discovered the mines of Potosí in Bolivia, thanks to information provided by one of the locals. The Spaniards immediately began to exploit the mines intensively, and huge quantities of silver were flowing to Europe on a regular basis by the second half of the 16th century.

Kinship played an important role in the organization of social groups. The dictionaries of the Quechua language, written by missionaries in the 16th and 17th centuries, went into great detail about the terminology of kinship in an attempt to define the degrees of consanguinity. For instance, the same term designated a great-grandfather and a great-grandson, indicating the cyclical nature of the Inca concept of time. Below: an Inca wedding, from a coloured engraving of 1820.

Mount Potosí, which was bursting with so much silver that it appeared inexhaustible, was transformed into a truly awful place: the tunnels were dug at an altitude of 5000 m, their gaping mouths in the iridescent slopes looking as if they wanted to swallow up this ghostly landscape. What else but poverty and the lure of gain could explain the extraordinary expansion that this place was to undergo during the colonial period? Adventurers, natives at odds with their communities, merchants, nouveau riche of mixed race, lords who had joined the bourgeoisie, financial backers, cooks and prostitutes would all turn this sinister region into a living urban centre, endowed with twenty-five churches and linked to the economic expansion of the West.

Most Inca gold was procured by panning rather than mining. Stone dams were built across rivers and gold particles collected from the stones, as in this Colombian engraving (above).

The *minero*, the man who found a seam, could either work it directly or rent it out, though on condition that one-fifth of the profits were reserved for the Crown.

In principle, anybody can become a *minero*. But in reality, working a seam is too costly for the native labour force to practise this trade

Work in the mines was carried out partly by the forced labour of the *mit'a*, and partly by free workers who were paid in kind, not in money. One cannot really talk of a salaried class. The freedom of these miners was quite relative: in order to meet their basic needs, the majority of them had to get into debt, mostly for life, to the owner of the seam.

The working conditions in these tunnels were inhuman. Forced to work without a break, some miners died of exhaustion underground before they could get out into the fresh air. Some seams were accessible only to children, who were made to crawl through cracks in the rock. Their parents sometimes preferred to deform one of their legs at birth, since lameness would exempt them from the obligatory service.

If the exploitation of these sites was profitable, and even enabled the Spaniards to accumulate substantial fortunes for more than two hundred years, it was due not so much to the quality of the mineral as to the existence of an abundant, cheap workforce subject to ruthless discipline.

Unusually, the extraction of precious metals in the Andean countries went hand in hand with very limited monetary circulation, while the natural economy was not undercut by the produce of the mines; we must look to the economists to explain this paradox.

When the Spaniards discovered the rich veins of silver at Potosí in Bolivia (below), they tapped this new source in a way that had never been attempted under the Incas, exploiting the natives as slave labourers. The shrine at the top of the mountain held one of the most famous Virgins in the empire.

Using repression one moment and persuasion the next, the 17th-century Spaniards were bent on destroying the rites and beliefs of the indigenous people. By cutting the Inca dynasties off from their ancestral roots in this way, the conquerors brought about an irreparable break between former times and colonial society.

CHAPTER 4

THE ERADICATION OF IDOLATRY

To bring the Indians to Christ was one of the major objectives of the conquest, undertaken in large measure by Franciscan friars (left). Indian ideas of Christianity, however, retain a strange ambivalence. Archangels were imagined as armed Spanish grandees with wings (right).

A lawyer by training, Polo de Ondegardo arrived in the Andes in the mid-16th century, a time when the whole country was still troubled by the revolt of the *encomenderos*. Appointed *corregidor* (magistrate) of Cuzco, and then of Potosí, two towns of primary importance to the government of the viceroyship, Polo de Ondegardo was to play a key role in the campaign against native religious practices.

Even before his arrival, the Spaniards knew that the Incas venerated the remains of their ancestors. Dressed in fine fabrics, covered in jewels and surrounded by precious objects, these mummies had aroused the greed of the conquistadors, who unhesitatingly violated numerous tombs to steal the treasures they contained.

The Incas believed that the life force of humans did not disappear at their death, but that these spiritual beings gathered in the beyond, eating and drinking as if they were alive. Mummies of the Paracas culture (above) were wrapped in fine woven textiles (left). Below: feather headdress on a skull from the Nazca culture. Opposite: a pre-Inca cemetery on the coast near Lima.

Polo de Ondegardo was a politician, not an adventurer. By questioning the native worthies of Cuzco and probably making them promises of which we know nothing, he discovered the places where the mummies of the Incas were hidden, then had them removed from their funerary dwelling and destroyed by fire. This act was to have serious consequences, because the cult of the dead was of enormous importance in Andean societies: the benevolence of the ancestors was necessary for a good harvest, and the corpses (*mallqui*) delivered messages to the living, through an interpreter; the bodies of the ancients, and anything that touched them, also possessed therapeutic qualities.

In order to give some human form to the funerary bundles in which the body was wrapped, a false head was placed at the top. On some of these faces the eyes are represented by shells and the nose by a triangular piece of wood. Often the head wears a wig of plant fibres topped by a bonnet or even a turban.

Only family heads and important people have the privilege of being embalmed and are invested with the gift of clairvoyance

It seems that the internal organs were buried in a receptacle and the corpse filled with tar, then dried by the same method used for preserving potatoes and meat: that is, successively exposed to night frosts and the severity of the sun. The mummies, curled up in the foetal position, were not buried but placed in natural cavities, niches or caves.

During the important festivities linked to the farming calendar or the celebration of military victories, the mummies of the Incas were taken out of their resting place to be transported with great pomp into the temple of the Sun at Cuzco or on to the main square. Dressed in sumptuous garments, and seated on golden chairs as befitted their rank, they were placed side by side with the principal divinities. They were given food and drink, and people danced before them. This cult of the ancestors was onerous, because in order to provide food for these mummies, land was set aside, the upkeep of which required a considerable workforce as well as tributaries who were compelled to take it in turns to work in these fields.

Indeed in the final years of his reign, the Inca Huascar, brother and enemy of Atahualpa, wanted to suppress the

cult of the mummies, which was far too costly a burden to bear. But he ran up against the hostility of the noble families, and this may be what brought him an ignominious death: he perished by drowning in the Andamarca River, and was hence deprived of immortality.

In the early years of the conquest, the Spaniards tried in vain to make Christian burial obligatory; but the local communities exhumed their dead in secret and took them back to their funerary niches, because they believed the deceased would suffer from the weight of the earth. However, little by little, the priests succeeded in instilling in their wards a fear of the next world and of ghosts – wandering souls without a grave who would take revenge on the living by inflicting illnesses on them. So the Catholic funerary rite finally won, but the Andean peasants have retained the custom, after the death of a

The bodies of the Incas and those lords worthy to remain in human memory were buried with great ceremony (below), and precious vessels (such as those above) were placed in their graves.

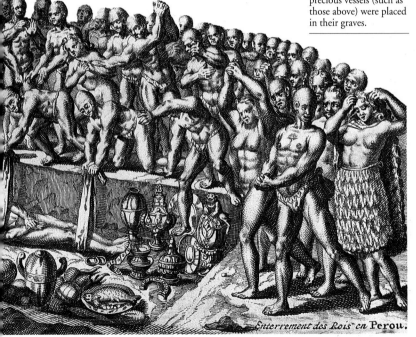

Enterrement des Rois en Perou.

The Bishop of Trujillo and an abbess (left). The imposition of ecclesiastical discipline and the foundation of religious orders were among the main objectives of the conquerors.

A 16th-century engraving of Cuzco (below).

relative or a neighbour, of washing themselves in a river along with all the deceased's possessions, to purify themselves from the taint of death.

Polo de Ondegardo discovers that the places of veneration, *huacas*, were laid out in accordance with astronomical and sociological factors

In fact, the term *huaca* refers to a number of very different things: holy sites, monuments, spirits of the air, and statuettes. The Incas aligned the sites along imaginary axes or *ceques* which radiated out from the city of Cuzco in all directions. A similar system existed at other towns in the territory. Once they had discovered this sacred topography, the Spaniards were able to find the *huacas*. They then destroyed the ones made of natural or cut stones, and kept a close watch on the rites at those which could not be destroyed, such as mountains or wells.

Hunted down by the *encomenderos* and the priests, neglected by their *caciques* who preferred to compromise with the invader and take advantage of the situation, and disappointed by the weakness of Inca resistance at Vitcos, the inhabitants of central Peru began to display strange behaviour which troubled the Spaniards: they were seized by frenzies and convulsions. Abandoning the cultivation of their fields, the possessed individuals claimed to be inhabited by the *huacas* which felt they had been overlooked since the arrival of the Christians, and were wandering through the air. Emaciated and thirsty, the *huacas* were in search of the body of an animate person to enter, so as to speak through his or her mouth.

The convulsives thought of themselves as living *huacas*, and received offerings from the faithful. They delivered prophecies, and announced the return of the Inca and its inevitable corollary: the definitive disappearance of the Spaniards, together with their animals, their wheat, their weapons and their religion. Just over thirty years had passed since Atahualpa's execution, and the hope that he had sown in the hearts of his wives was reborn in those of his unfortunate tributaries, forced by the *huacas* to obey them or perish.

This millenarian movement, called *taqui onqoy* ('dance of the Pleiades' or 'illness dance') gradually faded away

A pre-Inca textile doll of the Chancay culture (above).

with the fall of the Inca state of Vitcos. But other unorthodox behaviour appeared here and there, under the form of syncretism. Despite the vigilance of the ecclesiastical authorities, these composite rites resisted repression.

The feast of Corpus Christi, for example, corresponded to that of the Sun, and the native peoples used this coincidence to make offerings to their *huacas*, which were hidden behind the figure of a saint or Christ.

Because Spanish depictions of Saint James so often showed him with thunder, the Andeans saw him as a Hispanic version of Thunder and Lightning, a cosmic being which had always been a subject of adoration

The native communities abandoned the old names and even began to give this Christian name to their baptized children, a fact which did not escape the priests who forced them to change James into the innocuous Diego.

Other ancient festivals, like that of La Citua, continue to be celebrated in remote places. During the reign of the Incas, this imposing rite took place in the month of August, when the first rains began to fall; its function was to banish illnesses and misfortune which, it was thought, were punishments for neglecting the Inca or the *huacas*. On these occasions, strangers were chased out of town along with all those who had any kind of deformity, a clear sign of misconduct – or of sin. Then men dressed in warrior costume would exhort evil to

Contemporary Andean folklore is filled with malevolent spirits. The Spanish chroniclers of the 16th century claimed that the ancient Peruvians had a conception of the devil, whom they called *supay*. Below: a 19th-century print of a festival at Lima.

leave the town. Grouped in four squadrons, they set off in the direction of each of the four quarters of the empire to strike their invisible enemy. Once they had reached the frontier of the territory of Cuzco, they washed in a river to purify themselves. In the evening they lit straw torches and waved them like slings. The festival lasted several days, and comprised numerous purification rites, the aim of which was not so much to eliminate all pathogenic or malevolent elements as simply to drive them away. Similarly, the Citua's aim was not to destroy evil but to push it out beyond the town's boundaries.

The second Council of Lima, held in 1567, established strict rules for effectively combating this 'idolatry'. This term (which the clergy coined by analogy with ancient paganism) designated Inca beliefs, rites, customs, cults and ceremonies as the many signs of the aberration into which

Although the religious authorities understood that the festivals had a religious significance, they did not ban them, but limited themselves to condemning their diabolical purpose.

EL OTA BO INGA
VIRACOCHAINGA

the devil had led the credulous natives. For idolatry, practised by the civilizations of the ancient world, was not a regression but a perversion of the spirit.

Many chroniclers feel that the Andeans had an intuition of God through Viracocha, a mythical figure who emerged from Lake Titicaca

Viracocha created the first men from clay prototypes, which he modelled himself, before being exiled from the world of the living by the ingratitude of his creatures. Under the influence of Christianity, this civilizing hero was to take on the traits of an apostle, or even of God himself, who had come to preach the good news in these lost Cordilleras.

The church of Santo Domingo (opposite), built on the ancient temple of the Sun in Cuzco, is particularly striking testimony to the syncretism between the ancient Inca religion and Christianity. Left: Inca Viracocha by Guamán Poma de Ayala.

The Sun, ancestor of the Incas, held the most important place in the pantheon of idolatry. The Cuzco dynasties imposed its cult on all the conquered peoples, and at Cuzco they built a temple devoted entirely to the worship of the Sun; known as the Coricancha, its doors were covered in gold, and like so many other cult shrines, the Coricancha was desecrated and plundered when the Spaniards arrived. Part of the wealth from these temples formed Atahualpa's ransom, and pillage took care of the rest. Such vandalism must be ascribed to the soldiers rather than the clergy, for the latter mostly contented themselves with transforming the pagan buildings into churches. For example, the foundations of the Coricancha, still visible today, are surmounted by the church of Santo Domingo.

In reality, the number of *huacas* was, if not infinite, at least very considerable, since each locality and kinship group had its own. The stars were also venerated and, in

A terracotta figurine (below).

certain regions, it was thought that every living being had its astral double. Moreover, the moon was seen as a woman, and each time there was an eclipse, the locals – believing it had been devoured by a jaguar or a snake – made a great racket to undo this catastrophe.

If the heavenly bodies, meteorological phenomena and certain aspects of nature and topography were considered as *huacas*, there were also small ones: worked stones or statuettes that families kept from generation to generation, which looked after the fertility of family members and their land. Finally, the term *huaca* is still applied to anything strange, such as twin births, a harelip or an individual born feet first. Such protean beings do not fit well with the Western definition of 'god'.

The clergy systematically destroy any object that could form part of an idolatrous cult or serve as a reminder of one

Feathers, ritual fabrics, conch shells (the musical instruments used in festivities) and even cradles fed the purifying pyres, while hymns were banned and protective stones were thrown into the water or simply smashed.

At sites in the mountains where the natives left offerings to appease the *huacas*, the priests would set up crosses. But the clergy themselves recognized that sometimes very violent storms would break out in the highlands and tear out these signs that 'the mountain did not tolerate'.

Just as they had always fought against the native funerary customs, the extirpators also set about controlling the other rites of passage: birth, puberty and

• In removing all these things not merely from their eyes but even more so from their hearts, with continual sermons and the catechism, it is to be very greatly feared that roots which are so deep and so ancient have not entirely been drawn up or torn out with the first ploughing, and in order to prevent them growing again, to uproot them definitively, a second and third ploughing will be necessary. It is true that all the Indians visited remain informed, corrected and cured, and that the children will be better than their fathers, and the grandchildren better than their fathers and grandfathers....•

Pablo José de Arriaga, *The Extirpation of Idolatry in Peru,* 1621

French ballet costume of the age of Louis XIV (left), equating a priest of the sun with the Roi Soleil.

The dedication of Spanish priests eventually succeeded in completely suppressing the ancient religion, and today the Church in South America is among the most powerful in the world. Left: a priest gives absolution to a dying native. Above: sculpture of a musician playing a *quena*, a sort of clarinet.

marriage. In order to achieve a radical conversion of the native communities to Christianity, they had to bring about a total break with the past. So the clerical authorities forced the natives – not always successfully – to adopt new first names instead of the traditional names, suppressed the puberty ritual for boys of the nobility, and banned polygamy.

To enforce this cultural reform, the priests related edifying stories and used pictures that depicted the horrors of hell and the punishments of purgatory.

To replace the destroyed idols, the priests give out miraculous rosaries and images of Saint Ignatius with curative powers

Finally, they induced the converts to join religious confraternities protected by a saint. But the villagers managed to reconcile the practice of Christianity with their ancient mountain cults, and reconstituted, within the framework of the confraternity, the old kinship groups that had been disrupted by the Spanish reorganization of society. Although the Jesuits had eradicated a good number of idolatries, they had to resign themselves to tolerate a syncretic Catholicism that would survive into the 20th century.

In the eyes of the Jesuits, the 'ministers of the devil' were even more dangerous than objects. In this category they lumped the keepers of the *huacas*, healers, soothsayers, priests attached to the great temples, wizards and sorcerers, even though their roles were quite distinct: for example, a sorcerer was generally a malignant person who used poisoned food or manipulated objects with evil powers to induce death or terrible diseases – practices which had in fact been condemned by the Inca and incurred the death penalty. In reality, those bent on eradicating the old religion were perfectly aware of the difference between a herbalist, a keeper of mummies, a priest who performed sacrifices and a sorcerer, but they viewed them all with the same intolerant reprobation.

Among the characters the clergy most abhor are those who have the ability to understand the language of the *huacas*, and who can hence interpret the signs of nature and predict the future

These intermediaries between the invisible powers and humans were often chosen because of a particular personality trait. In a similar way, survivors of lightning strikes were thought to have powers of clairvoyance. To communicate with the *huacas*, the soothsayers used intoxicating substances such as *vilca*, a hallucinogenic plant of the genus *Banisteriopsis*. The intermediaries then uttered their prophecies in a special tone of voice,

The Spanish temperament had always been preoccupied with the paraphernalia of death, and in Central and South America they found peoples with curiously similar obsessions. The engraving opposite shows the festival of the dead at Cuzco.

Every community had to assign three of its number to the priest: a cook, a baker and a gardener. In addition, the priest received various payments: the tithes and first fruits, levied at harvest time; parish rights for the celebration of baptisms, marriages and funerals, as well as masses in honour of the saints (gifts that were theoretically voluntary); and a salary paid by the community. In this 19th-century painting a priest receives three women of Lima.

supposed to be that of the *huacas* speaking through their mouth. The muteness of the saints, whom the villagers identified as Christian *huacas*, struck them as odd, especially as they were represented in painting and sculpture with an absolutely terrifying realism. There were other important characters: the keepers of the *huacas*, for example, who organized public confessions during which people admitted their faults – such as not having respected the rites; not having made offerings to the *huacas* or the solar divinity; having profaned the chastity of the women reserved for the Inca; having killed or stolen; or, finally, having spoken ill of the Inca. Only the Incas and the Cuzco nobility confessed in secret.

Although this enumeration of faults inevitably evokes the Catholic practice of confessing sins, one should not forget that Inca society exercised draconian control over the population. And just as the ancient work discipline facilitated the adaptation of the native populations to the colonial system, so this traditional moral rigour made their conversion to Christianity easier.

In almost every society, those responsible for treating and curing illnesses enjoy great respect, and the Inca healers were no exceptions to this rule. However, judging from Quechua vocabulary for the parts of the human body, it seems that the anatomical knowledge of the Andean peoples was very limited. This did not prevent them from practising trepanation, however, which involved making small holes in the skull using very fine copper knives. Despite the dangerous nature of this operation, some patients at least must have survived, because skulls have been found in which the orifice had partially closed up again. As for bonesetters, who learned their art by treating themselves, they continued to practise in colonial Peru.

Far left: funerary doll of the Chancay culture. Left: painted textile from Nazca. In the imagery of the early Andean civilizations, the jaguar embodies a very ancient cult. At the time of the Incas this animal was associated with the lowlands and the savagery of the Anti Indians. In the coastal region near Trujillo, the jaguar filled the visions of sorcerers who supposedly sucked the blood of their victims like vampires.

Funerary masks such as the one above (from the Chancay culture) could be made of cloth, metal or even human skin, taken from a man of high rank.

Dance of the Lions (left), an Inca festival, from a 17th-century illustration. Above: the plains beneath the great volcano, Chimborazo, painted by Alexander von Humboldt.

To treat the most common illnesses, Inca medicine uses certain remedies of animal or mineral origin, as well as plants from different ecological zones

Itinerant healers, like the Bolivian *kallawaya*, travelled around the Andean provinces with their precious herbs and drugs.

The Spaniards took an immediate interest in these medicinal plants, because they too used herbal tonics for

the treatment of various maladies. European plants began to rival the native species in the 16th century, but even though the peasants gradually adapted these new species to their own needs, they continued to favour their existing pharmacopoeia; even the Europeans tended to prefer the indigenous remedies. The parish priests played an important role in extending this herbal medicine, because it was they who transcribed the recipes that circulated throughout the country. There were no rural doctors, despite the existence at Lima of a university with a good reputation.

In contrast to such therapeutic practices were those that touched on sorcery, designed to put an end to one's rivals. In the colonial period, Inca methods of sorcery were supplemented by other techniques brought in by the Spanish as well as the black slaves; these included dolls modelled in the image of one's enemy which were pierced with arrows to bring about his or her death. The Europeans circulated their books of spells, and enriched them with information obtained from the Andean peasants. It was widely believed that the *huacas* produced malevolent emanations that shrivelled the violators of tombs. It is probable that it was partly through medicine and sorcery that the different peoples coexisting in the Andes from the 16th century onward developed a common language.

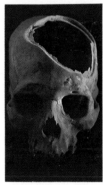

Trepanations were practised not only on living subjects but also on the dead, in order to pour substances into the skull that would preserve it from putrefaction.

Two hundred years after Pizarro's arrival, the Andean world was plunged into a profound misery, crushed by taxes and forced labour, and exasperated by the arrogance of the Spanish. There were rumblings of rebellion. The time had come to shake off the colonial yoke and restore the kingdom of the Incas.

CHAPTER 5

THE INCA'S RETURN

By a sort of retrospective iconography, this 17th-century representation of an Inca (left) shows him with the headdress of Atahualpa and the Sun symbol on his breast, but bearing the Christian cross. Right: a conquistador raises aloft his cross.

On their arrival in the Andes, the Spaniards had found a society that was hardworking, disciplined, even rigorous, but also strongly hierarchical. The ruling class was made up of powerful nobles, formerly in charge of independent provinces but now, following Inca expansion, vassals of the Inca himself. The lords of Chimor, Chincha, Lupaqa or Quito – all were at the head of important households. In the northern Andes these elites controlled the trade routes between the mountains and the lowlands; in the Lake Titicaca region they possessed immense herds of camelids; on the coast they were masters of the maritime trade and held the monopoly of the *mullu*, the sacred shell.

In return for their power, the lords had a certain number of obligations to fulfil, such as generosity towards their subjects and the redistribution of some of the resources that resulted from their position. Although hereditary, this position did not necessarily obey the rule of primogeniture (which the Spaniards were to impose later) and the seigneury could just as well be passed to a nephew – the son of the *cacique*'s sister, for example. The notion of private ownership of land did not exist before the colonial period; the wealth of the *caciques* was measured instead in terms of the numbers of houses, wives, servants and animals they held, together with ritual objects that in our eyes have no value, such as ornaments, bead necklaces, *keros* (vases used for ritual libations), feathers, little bells, shells, and, of course, large quantities of fabrics.

The nobles' servants or *yana* were either hereditary servants or slaves.

*K*eros were vases of gold or painted wood (as above) which the Incas used for their ritual libations. Of similar ritual significance were such symbols of power as feather crowns or fine fabrics (detail of a Paracas textile, left). Below: two pre-Inca vessels.

According to legend, these *yana* were formerly rebels against the Inca who had been reprieved by the *Coya*, his principal wife, and condemned to work for the lords or the state

In the Aymara kingdoms of Lake Titicaca, the *yana* watched over herds that numbered more than 20,000 animals and therefore required qualified pastors. Whether servants, serfs or herders, the *yana* were exempt from tribute and some even enjoyed real privileges, especially those who lived in the entourage of the Inca and his close relatives.

Nevertheless, the *yana* remained of inferior rank because, being detached from their native community and belonging to no particular territorial or kinship group, they were deprived of identity.

After the conquest, the *yana* kept their ancient privileges and were thus exempt from all forced labour. As they had no access to community land, however, they were forced to sell their manpower in the great domains

As well as traditional status objects, the *caciques* acquired Spanish furniture, including chests like this which bear witness to the emergence of a notion of private property, previously unknown among the Incas. They contained fabrics, Catholic liturgical objects, silks, title deeds and genealogies.

of the Spaniards, forming the nucleus of a servile workforce that was swelled through the centuries by a stream of natives driven by poverty to seek jobs in the haciendas.

Since the Spaniards belonged to a society founded on class distinctions, they respected the status of the Inca nobles and the *caciques*, though did not grant them any political autonomy. Pizarro lived maritally with two of Atahualpa's wives, first Doña Ines and then Doña Angelina by whom he had three children, one of them given the composite name of Francisco Pizarro Yupanqui. Other conquistadors took as wives women belonging to the Cuzco dynasties or the regional seigneuries. But while such unions with the indigenous elites undoubtedly took place, they never became common practice. On the other hand, the acculturation of the *caciques'* children was systematic from the 16th century onward; religious schools were established where they were taught the writing, language and manners of the Spanish nobility.

The *yana*, the Inca's appointed servants, became servants of the Spaniards in the colonial period, as in these 19th-century illustrations.

The *caciques* and their families dress in Spanish style, speak fluent Spanish and profess Catholicism

It was duty of the *caciques* to collect tribute and represent the indigenous community over which they exercised authority. For the Spanish authorities they were the indispensable intermediaries who could recruit a

There was a school in Cuzco for the children of the native nobility, run by the Jesuits. The twenty or so pupils dressed in Spanish style with a green uniform and a black hat. They wore their hair down to their shoulders, as a mark of their status: short hair was a mark of disgrace to the natives, and the missionaries often used this punishment to intimidate idolaters. The lessons consisted essentially of theology and doctrine. This picture shows members of the local community receiving religious instruction.

workforce. Their duties as go-between expedited their integration into the colonial world, and they often used their privileged position to acquire land and livestock, benefiting from the Hispanic law that regulated access to private property. In southern Peru and the region of Potosí in Bolivia, many of these officials became powerful merchants by monopolizing the mule traffic, for instance.

A

C

A... Yndio Principal de,
Quito trage de Gala.
B... Arbol de Guabas Macheronas, y,
Besuqillas.
C... Fagsos Fruta y el modo como se enreda
su rama
D... Arbol, y Fruta de las Guayabas.
E... Yndio del Campo.

Rural native

This native from the Yumbo tribe has hardly any of the attributes of Spanish civilization. His headdress, quiver and belt are adorned with feathers and he wears strings of shells round his neck and thighs. He is dressed for a feast (hence the colouring on his cheeks) and holds both a bow and a spear. The fruits include bananas, plantains and pineapples, 'very aromatic and tasty'. The painting typifies a certain view of colonial power, but should not be seen as a faithful image of social reality in 18th-century Peru.

A. Yndio Yumbo
de las immediaciones
de Quito con su trage
de Plumas y Cornillas de
Animales de Caza de que vsa
quando estan de Pala

B. Platano, Arvol que Produce
los de la Casta de Guineos con
su Fruto, y son los mas delicados.

C. Platano Arvol q̃ los Produce lla-
mados Dominicos, que no son de
tan delicado savor como los pri-
meros.

D. Arvol que Produce las Papaias,
y su Fruta entera y avierta, es
saludable.

E. La Piña consu Mata cuierta y entera, Es Fruta muÿ ôlorosa y
Gustosa

A... Yndia en trage de Gala.

B... Yndia del Canpo con su Faba Real.

C. Arbol de Aguacates, y su Fruta.

D. Arbol de chilguacanes con su Fruta entera, y partida.

E. Arbol de Chamburos con su Fruta entera, y abierta.

F. Mamey con sus ojas, y fruta abierta.

But the *caciques* remained torn between the two cultures since they preserved some features from the past, such as a defiant pride befitting the great lords of old; they liked to drink, though not to excess, and were ready to display enormous generosity. They were inordinately fond of ostentatious luxury, coats of arms and music, and they maintained ties of spiritual kinship with their subjects by means of patronage.

To limit the power of the *caciques*, the colonial administration created a parallel power within the indigenous villages, along the lines of the Spanish municipal council. At the head of this organization was the mayor (*alcalde*) who dealt with the distribution of land and kept a watchful eye on the conduct of the natives. Along with the *cacique*, he was responsible for collecting tribute, and was assisted by two *regidores* or municipal magistrates; finally, an *alguacil* acted as policeman. The members of the municipal council were elected annually. 'Commoners' – that is, peasants – could be candidates, but only on condition that they were good Christians and would cooperate with the Spanish authorities, because the councils were under the orders of the *corregidor*, a colonial magistrate at the provincial level.

The overlapping of administrative and religious authority is extremely close

This phenomenon, which is characteristic of the rural colonial world, wove solid ties between the village worthies and the parish priest. The prestige of the members of the municipal council, and of all those who wished to become members, depended on their participation in the cult of the saints: it was up to the *priostes* (those 'appointed' to a saint) to gather the money needed for the celebration of the festival. The more sumptuous the festivities, the greater the esteem enjoyed by its organizers.

The 17th-century clergy attempted to suppress the ancient festivals in order to wipe the tradition of the *huacas* from the memory of the indigenous people. These were replaced by others which borrowed from the past and intermingled customs of European origin.

Don Francisco de Arobe, a former slave who survived a shipwreck, had, with his brothers, become *cacique* of the Cayapa people of Esmeraldas (Ecuador). This picture, painted in Quito by a local artist, shows them dressed in Spanish style with the typical golden ornaments of the Andean people. Right: the bullfight, introduced into Peru by the Spanish.

Carnival festivities, for example, which are pagan by definition, were adopted very quickly by the peasants who gave them a very different form from those in the towns. Other celebrations had much in common with the theatrical performances highly prized in Baroque Spain, but were adapted to Inca practices. Bullfights and equestrian games were also a big hit. The ancient rituals became clandestine or gradually gave way to festival-spectacles which, in their turn, became fixed in folklore.

But the noise of the festivals was not enough to muffle the sound of anger that was growing throughout the country – for the burden of forced labour and the development of large domains at the expense of community lands had reduced the native populations to poverty.

Towards the middle of the 18th century rebellions against Spanish oppression break out throughout the Andean region, from Ecuador to Argentina

In the forest zones of Tarma and Jauja, in Peru, a certain Juan Santos Atahualpa was to fight the Spaniards for twenty years, from 1742 to 1761. He proclaimed that he had come to reconstitute the kingdom of the Incas with its native, mixed-race and black sons. He could count, he said, on the help of his kinsmen the English, who had promised him weapons, since political and commercial tensions had set the Spanish Crown against England. The latter was certainly keen to establish trading links with a continent whose resources were monopolized by Spain.

In the region of Huarochiri, locals who had rebelled against fiscal abuses threw the *corregidor* and his brother-in-law, who was with him, from the top of a cliff. At Quito, the frenzy even affected parishes which had always been considered peaceful until then.

But it was in southern Peru and the region of Potosí that the insurrection shook the foundations of the viceroyship. The rural masses were kept in a state of ignorance and degradation by the *corregidores* and the priests, while on the other hand certain *caciques* enjoyed the benefit of a refined education which was eventually to backfire on the oppressor. Thus José Gabriel Condorcanqui, the principal figure in the anti-Spanish insurrection, was a *cacique* from Tinta, a direct descendant via his mother of Felipe Topa Amaru, who had been executed by the viceroy Francisco de Toledo in 1572. Raised in a Jesuit college, Condorcanqui read Latin fluently and spoke Spanish just like a Spaniard.

Condorcanqui laid claim before a tribunal to the seigneury of Tinta, which came down to him from his ancestors. Then he took the name of Topa Amaru, to underline his descent from the murdered last Inca.

Administrative posts were filled by natives who were elected by their community rather than being members of the elite. Access to these posts was closely tied to the candidates' commitment to Christianity. In this way, the municipal system overlapped with a religious hierarchy. Left: an official takes part in a religious procession with two children dressed as angels. Below: an officer of the militia.

Topa Amaru II, a merchant and owner of a troop of mules, travels around the southern Andes without alarming the Spanish authorities

With his ally Tomas Catari, legitimate *cacique* of Chayanta, he carefully prepared the general insurrection. It broke out in 1780 and spread like lightning. The rebel armies numbered up to 80,000 natives, together with many mixed-race sympathizers. Topa Amaru's programme was certain to alarm the Spanish monarchy, since he planned to abolish the mining *mit'a* and forced labour in general, as well as to restore the Inca empire.

Topa Amaru challenged the political legitimacy of the Spanish, whom he considered usurpers. He denounced the bad *corregidores* – 'enemies of God, atheists, Calvinists and Lutherans, idolaters of gold and silver';

Fighting alongside the regular troops of revolutionary leaders José de San Martín and Simon Bolivar, native guerrillas played an important role in the struggles for the emancipation of Peru, which lasted from 1819 to 1824. In 1824, after several years of war, Bolivar signed an act of gratitude in favour of the guerrillas' descendants. Below: Bolivar and Santander on campaign in Llanos (Colombia).

he attributed their villainy to the baseness of their nature. But the peasants were soon abandoned by the townspeople who, although hostile to the Spanish monarchy, had no wish to join a movement that was radical and – worse still – native. In 1781 Topa Amaru was arrested and tortured.

The last Inca was to undergo a death even more horrible than that of his ancestor: after witnessing the execution of his wife and his son, and then of his companions, he had his tongue cut out, and was tied to four horses to be torn apart. But his body would not tear, and his persecutors were forced to have his head cut off. Finally, his limbs were severed and sent to the four centres which had fomented the rebellion: the punishment thus acknowledged the spatial structure of the empire of the Four Quarters.

Portrait of Simon Bolivar. The historical fact of crossbreeding constituted the starting point of Bolivar's political and social theories. 'Our people', he said, 'is a mixture of Africa and America rather than an emanation from Europe. The majority of Indians were exterminated. The Europeans mixed with Americans and Africans. Whereas we all have the same mother, our fathers are foreigners and differ in their origins and their blood, as well as in the colour of their skin, which places obligations of the highest importance upon us.'

The Spaniards' revenge is not assuaged by the Inca's death: his relatives, as distant as fourth cousins, were hunted down and murdered

It seems that the only survivors of this massacre were the nephews of Topa Amaru, who found refuge in Surinam. The 18th century ended with the most brutal repression that the native peoples had ever suffered. But the victory of the Spanish authorities was shortlived. A few decades later, the Creoles (the name given to the descendants of Spaniards born on American soil, who were looked upon as second-class compatriots by Madrid) organized a revolution against the Spanish monarchy. This uprising led to the emancipation of the old colonies: between 1822 and 1824, at the cost of some bloody wars, Gran Colombia, Peru and Bolivia won their independence.

The patriots were inspired by the ideals of the French Revolution, and wanted to grant citizenship to the indigenous people. The *Libertador* José de San Martín abolished forced labour in Peru in 1821, even before achieving final victory. But the new republican regime, being founded on the concept of the private ownership of land – which it considered to be the best means of tying men to their country – tolled the death knell of the indigenous communities, which gradually lost their legal status and could not resist the extension of the big domains. Deprived of community land, the villagers were driven to accept the exploitative conditions of the *concertaje* – a system which, more often than not, put them in debt for life. Having received an advance from his employer at the start, the *concierto* had to work on his employer's fields until he had repaid the debt, plus interest. The economic liberalism of the new Latin-American states was ultimately to turn the native Americans into a proletariat.

After the liberation of the province of the Río de la Plata, the future Argentina, José de San Martín (far left) led his army from Chile to Peru. In 1822 he entered Lima and set up a republican government, himself receiving the title of 'protector of Peru'. Bolivar was at Quito, from where he controlled the whole of the north. These two men were completely different. Bolivar, more ambitious than San Martín and doubtless a better politician, eventually emerged as the victor. Back in Lima, San Martín resigned, gave up rank, and set sail for Chile that very evening. Bolivar disembarked at Callao and the Congress gave him full authority to repel a Spanish offensive. At Lima Bolivar swore the independence of Peru (left). San Martín was to end his days in exile in France, where he died in 1850 at Boulogne-sur-Mer.

In the 19th century, adventurers, explorers and gold prospectors travelled around Peru, all trying to find Vitcos and Vilcabamba. But the two citadels of Inca resistance in the 16th century seemed to have mysteriously vanished. In 1911 Hiram Bingham, an American historian, set off in his turn to search for the phantom cities.

CHAPTER 6

THE HERITAGE OF THE INCAS

The Andes formed, and still form, a virtually impassable barrier, perhaps still concealing undiscovered cities such as Machu Picchu (left). Below: view of Cajambé.

Passionately interested in Latin America and an authority on the revolutionary leader Simon Bolivar, Hiram Bingham set out to travel from Lima to Buenos Aires on a mule, and thus to cover a large part of Inca territory. The prefect of Apurimac, a province close to Cuzco, told him of ruins lost in the mountains, which the natives called Choqquequirau, the 'cradle of gold'. Access to these ruins was extraordinarily difficult, because there was no bridge over the Apurimac River, and most of the area was covered by forest. Tempted by adventure, Bingham prepared an expedition in the hope of discovering at last the two forest refuges of the Inca Manco and his sons, who resisted the Spaniards until 1572. The information at his disposal was pretty thin and, moreover, contradictory: there were firstly the writings of the 16th-century chroniclers, including the Inca Titu Cusi himself, the son of Manco and brother of the unfortunate Topa Amaru I. Titu Cusi testified, in Spanish, to the struggle against the invaders of the last Incas, who had fallen back to the Amazonian piedmont. Another source, an Augustinian missionary named Father Antonio de Calancha, located Vitcos at a place where a white rock overhung a waterhole, near a temple of the Sun. These were pretty meagre clues with which to find the traces of an Inca city, buried under the tropical vegetation...

The slopes and eastern piedmont of the central Andes are mostly sheer and deeply cut by narrow valleys. The only natural passages are the rivers such as the Urubamba (above), but these are punctuated by impassable rapids and falls. The site of Machu Picchu was discovered and excavated by foreigners (at right, Hiram Bingham and his guide) only after prolonged effort and hardship.

Although Bingham is not the first explorer to seek Manco's capital – there were many others in the 19th century – he is the luckiest

In the village of Ollantaytambo, built beside the Urubamba River, the inhabitants were still living in Inca dwellings. Travelling through the region, Bingham found numerous remains. One day, after questioning locals who were working in the valley's sugar-cane plantations, he finally found – at a spot called Rosaspata – a white rock that overhung a spring with black waters, close to a temple of the Sun. This sinister place fitted Calancha's description. Bingham had found Vitcos.

This discovery encouraged him to undertake a difficult expedition into the eastern valleys. He was now certain that the remains of Rosaspata were not those of 'Vilcabamba the ancient', Manco's capital. Still collecting information from native plantation workers, he finally reached Choqquequirau, where he found a real fortress, with paved roads and buildings of stones that had been fitted together perfectly with no mortar, by means of a remarkable technique. Clearly, other visitors had been there before the American, since he discovered signatures engraved on the walls, including that of a Frenchman, Eugène de Sartigues, who had passed through in 1834.

When Hiram Bingham, on his return from this expedition, admitted to the prefect of Apurimac that he had found no gold, there was great disappointment, despite the prestige that the other discovery might bring him.

Interest in the Incas during this period revolves almost exclusively around the gold in their tombs. The greed of the republicans matches that of the conquistadors

Bingham persisted. He wanted to find the city of Vilcabamba which, according to the 16th-century chroniclers, must be even farther away – 'a little further along' as his local guides kept repeating. Listening to the craziest rumours, Bingham forced a path through the suffocating gorges, and climbed up to glaciers only to redescend into the Amazonian furnace.

Father Calancha reported that, near Vitcos, there was a 'white stone' from which a spring arose. There, the *huaca* called 'parantin' delivered his prophecies. The Augustinian friars declared war on the 'demon', and exorcised the rock. Bingham found just such a rock (right).

In the time of the Incas, the monumental fortress of Ollantaytambo (left) had several functions: besides watching over the Urubamba Valley and keeping a lookout for the sporadic incursions by forest tribes which the Incas always dreaded, it was an agricultural centre, like its neighbour Pisac. It probably also served as a residence for the Inca or his family, to judge by the quality of the buildings, water channels and sanctuaries. The style of its stonework suggests that Ollantaytambo was built in the second half of the 15th century.

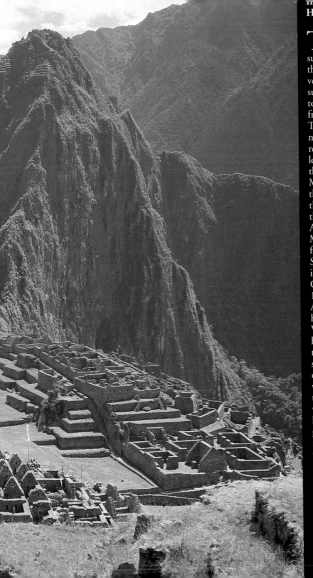

In the shadow of Huayna Picchu

The jagged contours of the mountain summit, together with the very dense vegetation that surrounded it, combined to isolate Machu Picchu from the outside world. The site was secluded not only from the Cuzco region but also from the lowlands – cut off by the gorge of the Pongo Moenike, impassable in the rainy season. Hence the remarkable nature of this urban settlement. According to legend, Machu Picchu was built for the virgins of the Sun, the *aclla*. For instance, Father Calancha reported in 1560 that two Augustinian friars, who had been invited to Vilcabamba by the Inca himself, underwent tough tests aimed at shaking their chastity: every evening, women were sent to tempt them, but apparently in vain. Nowadays, however, archaeologists give little credence to the idea that Machu Picchu was a shelter for his *aclla*; furthermore, most scholars identify Vilcabamba not with Machu Picchu but with Espiritu Pampa, a site the more hospitable environment of the headwaters of the Amazon.

After losing his way, he finally passed from the valley of the Apurimac, where the 'cradle of gold' stood, into that of the Urubamba. As he approached his goal, little by little, the locals' descriptions became more precise. The American was astonished by what appeared to be their indifference towards the ruins, ruins that should in his opinion have stirred their deepest emotions.

But to the inhabitants of the Andes, the archaeological remains inspired terrible fear. As a legacy of the 16th-century evangelists, the locals were especially fearful of human bones, which they had been led to believe could inflict appalling illnesses. Antonio Raimondi, pioneer of Peruvian archaeology, reports that the workers he employed in his excavations refused to unearth ancient tombs, out of fear of 'being crippled by the vapour of the corpses'.

After an arduous walk and an exhausting climb, Hiram Bingham reached his destination. The spectacle that met his eyes, one July day in 1911, was to compensate for all his pains: he had discovered Machu Picchu. He entered a magnificent city built on an eagle's nest where streets, staircases, monuments, temples, and houses were set in a sumptuous landscape. Opposite rose the peak of Huayna Picchu, which was also covered in ruins.

So is Machu Picchu Manco's city of Vilcabamba? So thinks Hiram Bingham, in his wonder at the perfection and beauty of its architecture

Machu Picchu had not been lost to everyone, to judge by the disorder in its tombs. Manco's treasure had disappeared. No one knew whether gold prospectors had pillaged it, or whether the last Inca, the young Topa Amaru, had taken part of his ancestors' riches away with him.

Instead of treasure, Hiram Bingham made other fascinating discoveries: besides the grandeur of the site, he was struck by the beauty of the construction of the stone monuments, which formed a unique group. No other civilization in the world had managed to assemble such enormous blocks so perfectly. The blocks were cut with bronze or stone tools, and the ridges rubbed

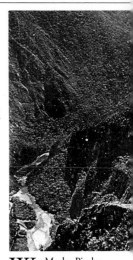

Was Machu Picchu a fortified post to control access to Cuzco? A kind of convent dedicated to the virgins of the Sun? The last refuge of the Inca Manco (the puppet ruler placed on the throne by the Spaniards who then revolted against his masters)? Few places can have inspired more hypotheses or interpretations than Machu Picchu; today it is the most visited site in South America. Above: view of Machu Picchu and the Urubamba Valley taken by Bingham; (right) the same valley as it is today.

‘Immediately in front, on the north side of the valley, was a great granite cliff rising 2000 feet sheer. To the left was the solitary peak of Huayna Picchu, surrounded by seemingly inaccessible precipices. On all sides were rocky cliffs. Beyond them cloud-capped, snow-covered mountains rose thousands of feet above us.’

Hiram Bingham, *Lost City of the Incas*, 1951

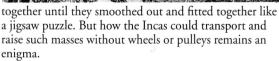

together until they smoothed out and fitted together like a jigsaw puzzle. But how the Incas could transport and raise such masses without wheels or pulleys remains an enigma.

Bingham found many two-storey houses with trapezoidal doors and windows, in a remarkable state of preservation. Perhaps the strangest monuments he stumbled upon were a rounded temple, probably consecrated to the Sun; a big square alongside which

Above: Inca houses were small and contained only one room and one door. Inside, trapezoidal niches were cut into the walls. Windows were rare. The beauty of the stonework contrasts with the smallness of the dwelling. Even today, the house is simply the place where one sleeps and seeks protection from the cold. Left: city gate of Machu Picchu as Bingham found it.

stood the 'temple with three windows'; and finally the *intihuatana* (which, in Quechua, literally means 'the hitching post of the sun'). The *intihuatana* is a kind of solar clock. It was here, at the winter solstice, when the sun declined and seemed to want to abandon humankind, that a priest performed a ritual aimed at tying the heavenly body to the stone, to prevent its disappearance. Machu Picchu's *intihuatana* only escaped the Spaniards' frenzy of destruction because it was so difficult to reach.

The discovery of this site marks the pinnacle of the neo-Inca craze that spread through Peruvian intellectual circles at the beginning of the 20th century

Peru had by this time been an independent country for a century. Like all new Latin-American states, it was in search of its identity. The indigenous people were too wretched for the elite that exploited them to recognize itself in them. On the other hand, the Incas – whose remains aroused great admiration throughout the world – acquired an emblematic value. With Bingham's discovery, they became a national symbol, which modern

Some structures were especially designed for astronomical observations, such as the *intihuatana* (above, at Machu Picchu) which were similar to sundials, and the *sucanca*, pillars set up to the east and west of Cuzco to measure solstices. The Incas believed that the Sun had two 'seats', the main one in the north and a secondary one in the south. The year began with the summer solstice, when the sun settled into its southern seat.

Peruvians could place beside any colonial form.

Can one speak of continuity between the Andean societies conquered by the Spaniards in 1532 and the indigenous peasants and proletariat of today? If one means biological or racial continuity, the answer can only be negative, with a few exceptions: racial intermixing, whether desired or simply accepted by the Spaniards, is an indisputable fact.

If one means cultural continuity, the answer is still disappointing for all those romantics who are fascinated by ancient grandeur. Evangelization, the transformation of the land system, the modification of the family structure and the suppression of indigenous authorities are all factors that have helped to forge a new identity for the peoples of the Cordilleras over the centuries. Nevertheless, despite these social upheavals, there is still such a thing as Andean culture, and it is quite unique. So, although it is pointless to want to detect unchanging survivals, one is compelled to note that neither those who sought to eradicate the old culture nor the administrators succeeded in turning the native population into Spanish labourers. The culture of the Andes is no more frozen in time than any other. It never ceases to integrate new elements, recreating and recasting them, ultimately elaborating a society that is like no other.

The Incas are not a fossilized people. Their image is still vivid in the minds of contemporary peasants who are excluded from all political power. Is this Inca image true to history, or does it serve a merely allegorical purpose? No matter. It lives in the hearts of those whom the modern world seems to have forgotten or rejected. And the memory of Inca resistance, from Manco to José Gabriel Topa Amaru, can still nourish dreams of rebellion.

Both political thinkers and poets have seen contemporary relevance in the Inca story. The Chilean poet Pablo Neruda, for example, wrote of Machu Picchu as the symbol of all Latin American peoples. But perhaps it is amongst the contemporary peasants that the collective memory of the Incas is kept most vividly alive.

DOCUMENTS

How can we find out about the life of
a civilization that has been so brutally
crushed? The writings of the conquistadors
and travellers, and accounts by the Inca
people themselves, all shed light on the
people of the Sun.

The conquistadors' testimony

The earliest chroniclers mainly describe the conquest of Peru and the civil wars between different factions of conquistadors. But from their own observations and the Indians' testimony they also relate the grandeur of the Inca empire and the ways and customs of its inhabitants. They were indisputably the first ethnologists of the modern era.

Francisco de Xeres was Francisco Pizarro's secretary. It was in Cajamarca (Caxamalca) that he wrote The Conquest of Peru *and gave the following description of the famous meeting between the conquistador and the Inca Atahualpa (Atabaliba).*

When the Governor saw that it was near sunset, and that Atabaliba did not move from the place to which he had repaired, although troops still kept issuing out of his camp, he sent a Spaniard to ask him to come into the square to see him before it was dark. As soon as the messenger came before Atabaliba, he made an obeisance to him, and made signs that he should come to where the Governor waited. Presently he and his troops began to move, and the Spaniard returned and reported that they were coming, and that the men in front carried arms concealed under their clothes, which were strong tunics of cotton, beneath which were stones and bags and slings; all of which made it appear that they had a treacherous design. Soon the van of the enemy began to enter the open space. First came a squadron of Indians dressed in a livery of different colours, like a

Pizarro's house in Cuzco.

chess board. They advanced, removing the straws from the ground, and sweeping the road. Next came three squadrons in different dresses, dancing and singing. Then came a number of men with armour, large metal plates, and crowns of gold and silver. Among them was Atabaliba in a litter lined with plumes of macaws' feathers, of many colours, and adorned with plates of gold and silver. Many Indians carried it on their shoulders on high. Next came two other litters and two hammocks, in which were some principal chiefs; and lastly, several squadrons of Indians with crowns of gold and silver.

As soon as the first entered the open space they moved aside and gave space to the others. On reaching the centre of the open space, Atabaliba remained in his litter on high, and the others with him, while his troops did not cease to enter. A captain then came to the front and, ascending the fortress near the open space, where the artillery was posted, raised his lance twice, as for a signal. Seeing this, the Governor asked the Father Friar Vicente if he wished to go and speak to Atabaliba, with an interpreter? He replied that he did wish it, and he advanced, with a cross in one hand and the Bible in the other, and going amongst the troops up to the place where Atabaliba was, thus addressed him: 'I am a priest of God, and I teach Christians the things of God, and in like manner I come to teach you. What I teach is that which God says to us in this Book. Therefore, on the part of God and of the Christians, I beseech you to be their friend, for such is God's will, and it will be for your good. Go and speak to the Governor, who waits for you.'

Atabaliba asked for the Book, that he might look at it, and the Priest gave it to

The Inca Atahualpa, drawn by Guamán Poma de Ayala.

him closed. Atabaliba did not know how to open it, and the Priest was extending his arm to do so, when Atabaliba, in great anger, gave him a blow on the arm, not wishing that it should be opened. Then he opened it himself, and, without any astonishment at the letters and paper, as had been shown by other Indians, he threw it away from him five or six paces, and, to the words which the monk had spoken to him through the interpreter, he answered with much scorn, saying: 'I know well how you have behaved on the road, how you have treated my Chiefs, and taken the cloth from my storehouses.' The Monk replied: 'The Christians have not done

A tahualpa is pulled off his litter by Pizarro, while his troops are slaughtered all around.

this, but some Indians took the cloth without the knowledge of the Governor, and he ordered it to be restored.' Atabaliba said: 'I will not leave this place until they bring it all to me.' The Monk returned with this reply to the Governor. Atabaliba stood up on the top of the litter, addressing his troops and ordering them to be prepared. The Monk told the Governor what had passed between him and Atabaliba, and that he had thrown the Scriptures to the ground. Then the Governor put on a jacket of cotton, took his sword and dagger, and, with the Spaniards who were with him, entered amongst the Indians most valiantly; and, with only four men who were able to follow him, he came to the litter where Atabaliba was, and fearlessly seized him by the arm, crying out *Santiago*. Then the guns were fired off, the trumpets were sounded, and the troops, both horse and foot, sallied forth. On seeing the horses charge, many of the Indians

who were in the open space fled, and such was the force with which they ran that they broke down part of the wall surrounding it, and many fell over each other. The horsemen rode them down, killing and wounding, and following in pursuit. The infantry made so good an assault upon those that remained that in a short time most of them were put to the sword. The Governor still held Atabaliba by the arm, not being able to pull him out of the litter because he was raised so high. Then the Spaniards made such a slaughter amongst those who carried the litter that they fell to the ground, and, if the Governor had not protected Atabaliba, that proud man would there have paid for all the cruelties he had committed. The Governor, in protecting Atabaliba, received a slight wound in the hand. During the whole time no Indian raised his arms against a Spaniard. So great was the terror of the Indians at seeing the Governor force his way through them, at hearing the fire of the artillery, and beholding the charging of the horses, a thing never before heard of, that they thought more of flying to save their lives than of fighting. All those who bore the litter of Atabaliba appeared to be principal chiefs. They were all killed, as well as those who were carried in the other litters and hammocks. One of them was the page of Atabaliba, and a great lord, and the others were lords of many vassals, and his Councillors. The chief of Caxamalca was also killed, and others; but, the number being very great, no account was taken of them, for all who came in attendance on Atabaliba were great lords. The Governor went to his lodging, with his prisoner Atabaliba, despoiled of his robes, which the Spaniards had torn off in pulling him out of the litter. It was a very wonderful thing to see so great a lord taken prisoner in so short a time, who came in such power. The Governor presently ordered native clothes to be brought, and when Atabaliba was dressed, he made him sit near him, and soothed his rage and agitation at finding himself so quickly fallen from his high estate. Among many other things, the Governor said to him: 'Do not take it as an insult that you have been defeated and taken prisoner, for with the Christians who come with me, though so few in number, I have conquered greater kingdoms than yours, and have defeated other more powerful lords than you, imposing upon them the dominion of the Emperor, whose vassal I am, and who is King of Spain and the universal world. We come to conquer this land by his command, that all may come to a knowledge of God, and of His Holy Catholic Faith; and by reason of our good object, God, the Creator of heaven and earth and of all things in them, permits this, in order that you may know him, and come out from the bestial and diabolical life you lead. It is for this reason that we, being so few in number, subjugate that vast host. When you have seen the errors in which you live, you will understand the good we have done you by coming to your land by order of his Majesty. You should consider it to be your good fortune that you have not been defeated by a cruel people, such as you are yourselves, who grant life to none. We treat our prisoners and conquered enemies with kindness, and only make war on those who attack us, and being able to destroy them, we refrain from doing so, but rather pardon them. When I had a Chief, the lord of an island, my prisoner, I set him free that henceforth he might be loyal; and I did the same with the Chiefs who were

lords of Tumbez and Chilimasa, and others who, being in my power, and deserving death, I pardoned. If you were seized, and your people attacked and killed, it was because you came against us with so great an army, having sent to say that you would come peacefully, and because you threw the Book to the ground in which is written the words of God. Therefore our Lord permitted that your pride should be brought low, and that no Indian should be able to offend a Christian.'

After the Governor had delivered this discourse, Atabaliba thus replied: 'I was deceived by my Captains, who told me to think lightly of the Spaniards. I desired to come peacefully, but they prevented me, but all those who thus advised me are now dead. I have now seen the goodness and daring of the Spaniards, and that Malçabilica lied in all the news he sent me touching the Christians.'

As it was now night, and the Governor saw that those who had gone in pursuit of the Indians were not returned, he ordered the guns to be fired and the trumpets to be sounded to recall them. Soon afterwards they returned to the camp with a great crowd of people whom they had taken alive, numbering more than three thousand. The Governor asked whether they were all well. His Captain-General, who went with them, answered that only one horse had a slight wound.

Francisco de Xeres
The Conquest of Peru, 1534
Translated by Clements R. Markham, 1872

Pedro Pizarro, cousin of Francisco the conquistador, was less than twenty years old when he was in Cajamarca. He wrote his account in 1571, and his information is less precise than that of de Xeres.

I shall relate the war between Atabaliba and Guascar [Huascar] as I heard it from many Indians and important Lords of this land. In this kingdom there were five Lords Incas before the era in which the Spaniards entered it. These began to conquer and rule this land, making themselves Kings of all of it, because before these Lords vanquished it all the land was divided into behetrias [independent tribes], although there were some Lords who had small peoples subject to their government, but these were few, and so the behetrias were ever bringing war the one against the other. These Indians say that an Inca arose [and became] the first Lord. Some say that he came forth from the island of Titicaca, which is an isle in a lake in the Collao which is seventy leagues in circuit, and in it, at times, there are storms as in the sea. A small fish, somewhat more than a palm long, is raised in the lake. The water is a little saltish. This lake drains into another which is formed in the province of Carangas and Quillacas, almost as great as this other [lake]. No outlet is to be found, nor [is it known] by what way it is drained. It must be understood to reach the sea by underground channels because, to judge by the great quantity of water which enters it, it can not be otherwise. Other Indians say that this first Lord came forth from Tambo. This Tambo is in Condesuios, six leagues, more or less, from Cuzco. This first Inca, so they say, was called Inca Vira Cocha. They say that he conquered, won and subjected to his rule the

Engraving of Topa Yupanqui, the tenth Inca.

country, for thirty leagues around Cuzco, where this first Inca established himself. This Inca Vira Cocha left one son who was called Topa Inca Yupanqui Pachacuti who, they say, won one hundred leagues, [as well as other sons] Guaina Inca and Inca Amaru Inca. And these two successors conquered as far as Caxamalca. Guaina Capa, who was the fifth descendant of these, went conquering as far as Quito, and his captains, in another direction, as far as Chile and as far as the bay of Sant Mateo, and it is almost a thousand leagues from one region to the other. These Lords had the custom of taking their own sisters as wives, because they said that no one was worthy of them save themselves. There was a lineage of these sisters who descended by the same line as these Lords, and the sons of these women were the ones who inherited the kingdom, always the oldest son. Then, besides these sisters, these Lords had all the daughters of the caciques of the kingdom for their concubines, and these waited upon the great sisters, and in number they were much more than four thousand. Thus all the Indian women who looked comely to them were divided into lots by these sisters who, themselves, were many....

While this Guaina Capa was conquering around Quito, they say he dallied in winning it [Quito] during more than ten years, and he had this Atabaliba by the daughter of the chief Lord of this province of Quito. Having finished the conquest, Guaina Capa commanded that a fortress be built in memory of the victory which he had won, and thus it was the custom to do in all the provinces which they gained. While they were engaged upon this work, there broke out among them a plague of smallpox, never seen among them before, which killed many Indians. And while Guaina Capa was shut up, engaged in the fast which he was wont to make, which took the form of being alone in a room without access to any woman, and without eating either salt or aji, with which they dress their food, and without drinking chicha (he was thus for nine days, at other times for three), while Guaina Capa was thus at his fast they relate that three Indians never seen before came in to him. They were very small, like dwarfs. They said to him: Inca, we are come to summon you. And when he saw this vision [and heard] this which they said to him, he cried out to his servants, and as they entered, these three [dwarfs] already mentioned disappeared, and no one saw them save Guaina Capa, and he said to his servants: Who are these dwarfs who came to summon me? And they answered unto him: We have not seen them. Then said Guaina Capa: I am about to die. And at once he fell ill of the smallpox. While he was thus very ill, they sent messengers to Pachacamac... and the demon spoke through the idol and bade them take him out into the

sun, and soon he would become well. Then, when they did so, matters went the other way, and on being placed in the sun, this Guaina Capa died. The Indians say that he was a great friend of the poor, and he ordered that great care should be taken of them throughout the land. They say that he was very affable to his servants, and very grave. They say that he was wont to drink much more than three Indians together, but that they never saw him drunk, and that, when his captains and chief Indians asked him how, though drinking so much, he never got intoxicated, they say that he replied that he drank for the poor of whom he supported many. And had this Guaina Capa been alive when we Spaniards entered this land, it would have been impossible for us to win it, for he was much beloved by all his vassals. Ten years had passed since his death when we entered the land. And likewise, had the land not been divided by the wars between Guascar and Atabaliba, we would not have been able to enter or win the land unless we could gather one thousand Spaniards for the task, and at that time it was impossible to get together even five hundred Spaniards on account of their scanty numbers and the evil reputation which the country had, as I have said.

Guaina Capa being dead, they raised up as Lord Guascar his son, to whom the kingdom [rightfully] belonged, and who was in Cuzco, for there his father...had left him. But after some years had passed by, and Atabaliba got his growth, and he was in Quito, where his father begot him, as has been said, he had become very manful and bellicose, and for this reason they advised Guascar to summon him and keep him by him [at court]. When Guascar sent to call him, Atabaliba replied to the messengers

HISTORIA GENERAL
DE LOS HECHOS
DE LOS CASTELLANOS
EN LAS ISLAS Y TIERRA FIRME
DEL MAR OCEANO
Escrita por Antonio de Herrera
Coronista
Mayor de SU MAGESTAD
de las Indias y Coronista de Castilla
y Leon
DECADA SESTA
AL REY *Nuestro Señor*

From the end of the 16th century onward, published accounts of the Spanish conquest became very popular.

of his brother [saying that], as he had to have an Inca there [in Quito] as a governor, they might say [to Guascar] that he [Atabaliba] was there [for the purpose]. Then, Guascar being counselled by his vassals not to allow it, lest he [Atabaliba] rise up in revolt, he [Guascar] sent a second time to summon him, and he replied in the same manner, and the third time he sent to call him he [Guascar] added that if he did not at once obey the orders given to him, he [Guascar] would send for him. The vassals he [Atabaliba] had in Quito through the family of his mother, as I have said, advised him to arise, as he was the Lord, and because, if he went to Cuzco, he would kill his brother, for he also was a son of Guaina Capa, like

Guascar, albeit a bastard in order to inherit the kingdom from those to whom it belonged, as I have related above, and [they said] that [the rightful heirs] would aid him and would make him the Lord, for it was known that the men of Quito were the most valiant Indians of this kingdom, as indeed they were. Atabaliba, seeing the will of his vassals, caused himself to be raised up as Lord over them and over the Cañares who aided him.

When Guascar received the news of the uprising of his brother Atabaliba, he sent his captains against him with warriors, and at Tomebamba there was a battle between the two forces, at which Atabaliba was made a prisoner by the men of Guascar, and after they had placed him in a house under guard, one night he broke loose, saying that the sun, who was his father, had set him free, and so do all these Lords declare that they were the sons of the sun. [In truth] it was on account of the insufficient guard which was put over him, for until midnight these Indians keep watch vigilantly, but from midnight onward they all go to sleep, and we Spaniards have seen this during our experiences while conquering the country, especially in the region of Cuzco. Having got free, Atabaliba set himself to re-forming his troops, and he went on ever victorious. These Indians say that the reason why Guascar was but little liked was that he was very grave, and he never let himself be seen by his people, nor did he ever come out to eat with them in the plaza, as it was the custom of former Lords to do sometimes, although others say that the chief reason which led to his downfall was that which I shall here set forth. These Lords had the law and custom of taking that one of their Lords who died

Atahualpa's army is pulverized by Pizarro at Cajamarca.

and embalming him, wrapping him up in many fine clothes, and to these Lords they allotted all the service which they had had in life, in order that these bundles [mummies] might be served in death as well as they had in life. Their service of gold and silver was not touched, nor was anything else which they had, nor were those who served them [removed from] the house without being replaced, and provinces were set aside to give them support ....

Returning now to Guascar, [it is said that] one day becoming angry with these dead people, he said that he was going to have them all buried, and was going to take away from them all that they possessed, and that there were to be no more dead, but only living, for they [the dead] had all that was best in his kingdom. Since, as I have said, the greater part of the chief people were with these [the dead] on account of the many vices which they had there, and they began to hate Guascar, and they say that the captains whom he sent against Atabaliba let themselves be conquered and that others deserted and passed over to him, and for this reason could Atabaliba conquer, for otherwise neither he nor his people were sufficient to vanquish a village, much less a whole kingdom, and so was Guascar taken prisoner, as I have said, by the captains of Atabaliba, and slain.

Pedro Pizarro
Relation of the Discovery and Conquest of the Kingdoms of Peru, 1571
Translated by Philip A. Means, 1921

The epic of the conquest

W.H. Prescott's History of the Conquest of Peru *(1847), is a masterpiece of 19th-century narrative history. Prescott had the imagination of a novelist and, without departing from the documentary records, he contrived to make the adventures of Pizarro come alive in his readers' minds. Here he describes the journey from the coast to Cajamarca.*

Pizarro is welcomed to Cuzco.

At early dawn the Spanish general and his detachment were under arms, and prepared to breast the difficulties of the sierra. These proved even greater than had been foreseen. The path had been conducted in the most judicious manner round the rugged and precipitous sides of the mountains, so as best to avoid the natural impediments presented by the ground. But it was necessarily so steep in many places, that the cavalry were obliged to dismount, and, scrambling up as they could, to lead their horses by the bridle. In many places, too, where some huge crag or eminence overhung the road, this was driven to the very verge of the precipice; and the traveller was compelled to wind along the narrow ledge of rock, scarcely wide enough for his single steed, where a mis-step would precipitate him hundreds, nay, thousands, of feet into the dreadful abyss! The wild passes of the sierra, practicable for the half-naked Indian, and even for the sure and circumspect mule – an animal that seems to have been created for the roads of the Cordilleras – were formidable to the man-at-arms, encumbered with his panoply of mail. The tremendous fissures, or *quebradas*, so frightful in this mountain chain, yawned open, as if the Andes had been split asunder by some terrible convulsion, showing a broad expanse of the primitive rock on their sides, partially mantled over with the spontaneous vegetation of ages; while their obscure depths furnished a channel for the torrents, that, rising in the hearts of the sierra, worked their way gradually into light, and spread over the savannas and green valleys of the *tierra caliente* on their way to the great ocean.

Many of these passes afforded obvious points of defence; and the Spaniards, as they entered the rocky defiles, looked with apprehension lest they might rouse some foe from his ambush. This apprehension was heightened, as, at the summit of a steep and narrow gorge, in which they were engaged, they beheld a strong work, rising like a fortress, and frowning, as it were, in gloomy defiance on the invaders. As they drew near this building, which was of solid stone, commanding an angle of the road, they almost expected to see the dusky forms of the warriors rise over the battlements, and to receive their tempest of missiles on their bucklers; for it was in so strong a position, that a few resolute men might easily have held there an army at bay. But they had the satisfaction to find the place untenanted; and their spirits were greatly raised by the conviction that the Indian monarch did not intend to dispute their passage, when it would have been easy to do so with success.

Pizarro now sent orders to his brother to follow without delay; and, after refreshing his men, continued his toilsome ascent, and before nightfall reached an eminence crowned by another fortress, of even greater strength than the preceding. It was built of solid masonry, the lower part excavated from the living rock, and the whole work executed with skill not inferior to that of the European architect.

Here Pizarro took up his quarters for the night. Without waiting for the arrival of the rear, on the following morning he resumed his march, leading still deeper into the intricate gorges of the sierra. The climate had gradually changed, and the men and horses, especially the latter, suffered severely from the cold, so long accustomed as they had been to the sultry climate of the tropics. The vegetation also had changed its character; and the magnificent timber which covered the lower level of the country had gradually given way to the funereal forest of pine, and, as they rose still higher, to the stunted growth of numberless Alpine plants, whose hardy natures found a congenial temperature in the icy atmosphere of the more elevated regions. These dreary solitudes seemed to be nearly abandoned by the brute creation as well as by man. The light-footed vicuña, roaming in its native state, might be sometimes seen looking down from some airy cliff, where the foot of the hunter dare not venture. But instead of the feathered tribes whose gay plumage sparkled in the deep glooms of the tropical forests, the adventurers now beheld only the great bird of the Andes, the loathsome condor, who, sailing high above the clouds, followed with doleful cries in the track of the army, as if guided by instinct in the path of blood and carnage.

At length they reached the crest of the Cordillera, where it spreads out into a bold and bleak expanse with scarce the vestige of vegetation, except what is afforded by the *pajonal*, a dried yellow grass, which, as it is seen from below, encircling the base of the snow-covered peaks, looks, with its brilliant straw-colour lighted up in the rays of an ardent sun, like a setting of gold round pinnacles of burnished silver. The land was sterile, as usual in mining districts, and they were drawing near the once famous gold quarries on the way to Caxamalca. Here Pizarro halted for the coming up of the rear. The air was sharp and frosty; and the soldiers, spreading their tents, lighted fires, and, huddling round them, endeavoured to find some repose after their laborious march.

William H. Prescott
History of the Conquest of Peru, 1847

An Inca's account of everyday life

Garcilaso de la Vega, author of The Royal Commentaries of the Incas *(1609), was the son of an Inca princess and a Spanish captain. Although his view of Inca justice is somewhat idealized, his recollections constitute an authentic testimony of the world of the ancient Incas.*

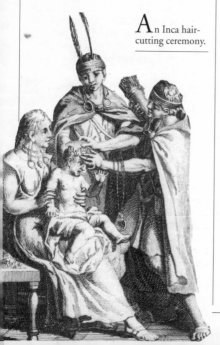

An Inca hair-cutting ceremony.

How their children were brought up without any care

Their children were strangely brought up, both those of the Incas and those of the people, whether rich or poor, without any distinction, and with as little care as could be bestowed upon them. As soon as a child was born, they bathed the little creature with cold water before wrapping it in a blanket; and each morning, before it was wrapped up, they washed it with cold water, generally in the open air. And when the mother would show unusual tenderness, she took the water in her mouth and washed the whole of the child's body with it, except the head, and particularly the crown of the head, which they never touched. They said that they did this to accustom the children to the cold and to hard work, and also to strengthen their limbs. They did not loosen the children's arms from the swaddling bands for more than three months, saying that if they were loosened before that time, the arms would become weak. They were always kept tied up in their cradles, which were benches badly made, four feet long, and one foot was shorter than the others, that the child might be able to rock. The seat or litter, on which they put the child was made of a thick net, as strong as a board, and the same net went round each side of the cradle, that the child might not fall out.

Neither in giving them milk, nor at any other time, did they ever take them in their arms, for they said that this would make them cry, and want always to be in their mothers' arms and never in their cradles. The mother leant over her child and gave it the breast, and this was done three times a day, in the morning, at noon, and in the evening.

They did not give the child milk at any other time, even if it cried, for they said that if they did it would want to be sucking all day long, and become dirty with vomitings, and that when it was a man it would grow up a great eater and a glutton. The animals, they said, did not give milk to their young all day long, but only at certain hours. The mother herself brought up her child, and she was not allowed to give it out to nurse, how great lady so-ever she might be, unless she was suffering from illness; and while she was suckling the child she abstained from sexual relations with her husband, because they said it was bad for the milk, and made the child pine away. They called those who had thus pined away *ayusca*, which is the past participle, and means literally the incapable, or more properly the changeling....

If the mother had sufficient milk to nourish the child, she never gave it any other food until it was weaned, because they said it injured milk; and they kept the children dirty and untidy. When it was time to take the children out of the cradle, in order not to have to carry them, they made holes in the ground, and put the children into them up to their breasts, wrapping them in dirty napkins, and putting a few trifles before them to play with. There they put the child to jump and kick, but they never carried it in their arms, even if it was a son of the greatest Curaca [native leader] in the kingdom.

When the child could crawl on all fours, it went to one side or the other of its mother to take the breast, and sucked with its knees on the ground, but it was not allowed to get on her lap. And when it wanted the other breast, it had to go round, that the mother might not be obliged to take it in her arms. The mother cared less about child-bearing than about nursing, for in giving birth she went to a stream, or washed with cold water in the house, and washed the house; beginning immediately afterwards to concern herself about her household affairs, as if nothing had happened. They gave birth without the aid of a midwife, and if such a person was ever used, she was more of a sorceress than a midwife. This was the usual custom of the Indian women in Peru, in bearing and nursing their children, without distinction between rich and poor, high and low....

How they counted by strings and knots, and the great accuracy of their accountants

Quipu means to knot, or a knot, and it was also understood as an account, because the knots supplied an account of everything. The Indians made strings of various colours. Some were all of one colour, others of two combined, others of three, others more; and these colours, whether single or combined, all had a meaning. The strings were closely laid up in three or four strands, about the girth of an iron spindle, and three quarters of a *vara* long [c. 2 ft]. They were strung on a thicker cord, from which they hung in the manner of a fringe. The thing to which a string referred was understood by its colour: for instance, a yellow string referred to gold, a white one to silver, and a red one to soldiers.

Things which had no colour were arranged according to their importance, beginning with that of most consequence, and proceeding in order to the most insignificant; each under its generic head, such as the different kinds of grain under corn, and the pulses in the same way. We will place the cereals

The *quipu*, made of knotted strings, was used for keeping accounts.

and pulses of Spain in their order, as an example. First would come wheat, next barley, next beans, next millet. In the same way when they recorded the quantity of arms. First they placed those that were considered most noble, such as lances, next darts, next bows and arrows, then shields, then axes, and then slings. In enumerating the vassals they first gave the account of the natives of each village, and next of those of the whole province combined. On the first string they put only men of sixty and upwards, on the second those of fifty, on the third those of forty, and so on down to the babies at the breast. The women were counted in the same order.

Some of these strings had other finer ones of the same colour attached to them, to serve as supplements or exceptions to the chief record. Thus, if the main string of men of a certain age had reference to the married people, the supplementary string gave the number of widowers of the same age in that year. For these accounts were made up annually, and only related to one year. The knots indicated units, tens, hundreds, thousands, and tens of thousands, but they rarely or never went beyond that; because each village was taken by itself, and each district, and neither ever reached to a number beyond tens of thousands, though there were plenty within that limit. But if it was necessary to record a number equal to hundreds of thousands, they could do it, for in their language they were able to express any number known in arithmetic; but as they had no occasion to go beyond tens of thousands, they did not use higher numbers. These numbers were counted by knots made on the threads, each number being divided from the next. But the knots for each number were made together in one company, like the knots represented on the girdle of the ever blessed Patriarch St. Francis; and this could easily be done as there were never more than nine, seeing that the units, tens, etc., do not exceed that number. On the uppermost knot they put the highest number, which was the tens of thousands, on the next below the thousands, and so on to the units. The knots of each number, and each thread, were placed in a line with each other, exactly in the way a good accountant places his figures to make a long addition sum. These knots or *Quipus* were in the charge of Indians who were called *Quipu-camayu*, which means 'He who has charge of the accounts'. Although there was, at that time, little difference of character among the Indians, because owing to their gentle dispositions and excellent government all might be called good, yet

the best, and those who had given the longest proofs of their fitness, were selected for these and other offices. They were not given away from motives of favouritism, because these Indians were never influenced by such considerations, but from considerations of special fitness. Not were these either sold or farmed out, for they knew nothing of renting, buying, or selling, having no money. They exchanged one article of food for another, and no more; for they neither sold clothes, nor houses, nor estates.

The *Quipu-camayus* being so trustworthy and honest, as we have described, their number was regulated according to the population in each village; for, however small the village might be, there were four accountants in it, and from that number up to twenty or thirty; though all used the same register. Thus, as only one account was kept, one accountant would have been sufficient; but the Incas desired that there should be several in each village to act as checks upon each other, and they said that where there were many all must be in fault or none....

The Inca Pachacutec increased the schools and made laws for their good government

The Father Blas Valera, speaking of this Inca, says as follows: 'The Inca Huiraccocha being dead and worshipped among the Indians as a god, his son, the great Titu, with surname of Manco Ccapac, succeeded him. This was his name until his father gave him that of Pachacutec, which means "Reformer of the World". That title was confirmed afterwards by his distinguished acts and sayings, insomuch that his first name was entirely forgotten. He governed his

M anco Capac, first Inca and founder of the dynasty.

empire with so much industry, prudence and resolution, as well in peace as in war, that not only did he increase the boundaries of all the four quarters, called *Ttahua-ntin-suyu*, but also he enacted many laws, all which have been confirmed by our Catholic kings, except those relating to idolatry and to forbidden degrees of marriage. This Inca above all things ennobled and increased, with great privileges, the schools that were founded in Cuzco by the King Inca Rocca. He added to the number of the masters, and ordered that all the lords of vassals and captains and their sons, and all the Indians who held any office, should speak the language of Cuzco; and that no one should receive any office or lordship who was not well acquainted with it. In order that this useful law might have full effect, he appointed very learned masters for the sons of the princes and nobles, not only for those in Cuzco, but also for those throughout the provinces, in which he stationed masters that they might teach the language of Cuzco to all who were employed in the service of the state. Thus it was that in the whole empire of Peru one language was spoken, although now (owing to negligence) many provinces, where it was once understood, have entirely lost it, not without great injury to the preaching of the gospel. All the Indians who, by obeying this law, still retain a knowledge of the language of Cuzco, are more civilized and more intelligent than the others.'

'This Pachacutec prohibited any one, except princes and their sons, from wearing gold, silver, precious stones, plumes of feathers of different colours, nor the wool of the vicuña, which they weave with admirable skill. He permitted the people to be moderately ornamented on the first days of the month, and on some other festivals....'

Many other laws of the Inca Pachacutec, and his sententious sayings

'In fine this King, with the advice of his Council, made many laws, rules, ordinances, and customs for the good of the people in numerous provinces. He also abolished many others which were detrimental either to the public peace or to his sovereignty. He also enacted many statutes against blasphemy, patricide, fratricide, homicide, treason, adultery, child-stealing, seduction, theft, arson; as well as regulations for the ceremonies of the temple. He confirmed many more that had been enacted by the Incas his ancestors; such as that sons should obey and serve their fathers until they reached the age of twenty-five, that none should marry without the consent of the parents, and of the parents of the girl; that a marriage without this consent was invalid and the children illegitimate; but

The teaching methods of the evangelists, condemned by the Inca Guamán Poma de Ayala.

that if the consent was obtained afterwards the children then became legitimate. This Inca also confirmed the laws of inheritance to lordships according to the ancient customs of each province; and he forbade the judges from receiving bribes from litigants. This Inca made many other laws of less importance, which I omit, to avoid prolixity. Further on I shall relate what laws he made for the guidance of judges, for the contracting of marriages, for making wills, and for the army, as well as for reckoning the years. In our time the Viceroy, Don Francisco de Toledo, changed or revoked many laws and regulations made by this Inca; and the Indians, admiring his absolute power, called him the second Pachacutec, for they said he was the Reformer of the first Reformer. Their reverence and veneration for this Inca was so great that to this day they cannot forget him.'

Down to this point is from what I found amongst the torn papers of Father Blas Valera. That which he promises to write further on, touching the judges, marriages, wills, the army, and the reckoning of the year, is lost, which is a great pity....

Of the precious leaf called *cuca*, and of tobacco

It would not be reasonable to forget the plant which the Indians call *cuca* and the Spaniards *coca*. This plant has been and is the principal wealth of Peru, for those who are engaged in trade. It is, therefore, right to give a complete account of it, seeing that it is esteemed so highly by the Indians for its many and great virtues known to them in old times, and for many more which the Spaniards have discovered, in regard to its medicinal uses. The Father Blas Valera, as a close observer, and one who resided many years in Peru and left it more than thirty years after my departure, writes of both the one and the other class of virtues, as one who had tried them. I will first give what his Paternity says, and then add the little that remains to be told. He says:

'The *cuca* is a small bush of the height and thickness of a vine. It has few branches, and on them many delicate leaves of the width of the thumb, and as long as half a thumb's length. They are of a pleasant smell, but not soft. These leaves are called *cuca*, both by Indians and Spaniards. The Indians are so fond of the *cuca* that they prefer it to gold, silver, and precious stones. They

cultivate it with great care and diligence, and are even more careful in getting in the crop. They pick the leaves, one by one, by hand, and dry them in the sun. But they do not swallow the leaves. They merely enjoy the flavour, and pass out the juice. It may be gathered how powerful the *cuca* is, in its effect on the labourers, from the fact that the Indians who use it become stronger and much more satisfied, and work all day without eating. The *cuca* preserves the body from many infirmities, and our doctors use it pounded, for applications to sores and broken bones, to remove cold from the body, or to prevent it from entering, as well as to cure sores that are full of maggots. If it is so beneficial and has such singular virtue in the cure of outward sores, it will surely have even more virtue and efficacy in the entrails of those who eat it? It has another important use, which is that the greater part of the revenue of the bishops and canons of the cathedral of Cuzco is derived from the tithe of the *cuca* leaves; and they enrich many Spaniards who trade with them. But some people, ignoring all these virtues, have said and written many things against the little plant, with no other reason than that the gentiles, in ancient times, and now some wizards and diviners, offered *cuca* to the idols, on which ground these people say that its use ought to be entirely prohibited....'

Thus far is from Blas Valera. To add a few more particulars, we will first remark that these little plants are about the height of a man, and, in planting them, they put the seeds into nurseries, in the same way as with garden stuffs, but drilling a hole as for vines. They layer the plants as with a vine. They take the greatest care that no roots, not even the smallest, be doubled, for this is sufficient

As in the past, coca is transported in bundles of dried leaves.

to make the plant dry up. When they gather the leaves, they take each branch within the fingers of the hand, and pick the leaves until they come to the final sprout, which they do not touch, lest it should cause the branch to wither. The leaf, both on the upper and under side, in shape and greenness, is neither more nor less than that of the arbutus, except that three or four leaves of the *cuca*, being very delicate, would make one of an arbutus in thickness. I rejoice to be able to find things in Spain which are appropriate for comparison with those of that country, that both here and there people may know one by another. After the leaves are gathered, they put them in the sun to dry. For they lose their green colour, which is much prized, and break up into powder, being so very delicate, if they are exposed to damp in the *cestos* or baskets in which they are carried from one place to another. The baskets are made of split canes, of which there are many of all sizes in these provinces of the Antis. They cover the outside of the baskets with the leaves of the large cane,

which are more than a *tercia* wide, and about half a *vara* long, in order to preserve the *cuca* from the wet; for the leaves are much injured by damp. The basket is then enveloped by an outer net made of a certain fibre. In considering the number of things that are required for the production of *cuca*, it would be more profitable to return thanks to God for providing all things in the places where they are necessary, than to write concerning them, for the account must seem incredible. They gather the *cuca* leaves every four months, which makes three harvests a year. If the ground is weeded well and thoroughly of the numerous herbs that continually spring up, by reason of the warmth and dampness of the climate, each harvest may be anticipated by more than a fortnight, which makes nearly four harvests in the year....

Of the plant which the Spaniards call tobacco, and the Indians *sayri*, we shall speak in the other part. Doctor Monardo writes wonders concerning it. The *sarsaparilla* needs no praise from anyone; for its own deeds are its sufficient praise, both in the Old World and the New, in curing bubos and other grave infirmities. There are many other herbs in Peru of such virtue as medicines that, as Father Blas Valera says, if they were all known it would be unnecessary to bring any from Spain, or from anywhere else. But the Spanish doctors think so little of them, that even those that were formerly known to the Indians, are, for the most part, forgotten.

Inca Garcilaso de la Vega
The Royal Commentaries of the Incas, 1609, 1617
Translated by Clements R. Markham, 1869–71

Rites and religion in the Old World

The Inca calendar was punctuated by a series of festivals. Most of these either celebrated major events in the agricultural cycle – for instance sowing, the first rains, or harvest – or corresponded with various points in the astronomical calendar, such as the solstices or equinoxes.

A native band with drums and pan-pipes.

The following extract comes from The Fables and Rites of the Incas *by Christobal de Molina, published in 1573. The work is an important one, for Molina had a good understanding of the Quechua language and was thus able to obtain first-hand accounts from native chiefs and learned men of Inca religious practices before the conquest. Here he describes the festival of the Situa (Citua) which took place in August.*

The month of August was called Coya-raymi; and in it they celebrated the *Situa*. In order to perform the ceremonies of this festival, they brought the figures of their huacas from all parts of the land, from Quito to Chile, and placed them in the houses they had in Cuzco, for the purpose which we shall presently explain. The reason for celebrating the feast called *Situa*, in this month, was, because the rains commenced, and with the first rains there was generally much sickness. They besought the Creator that, during the year, he would be pleased to shield them from sickness, as well as in Cuzco, as throughout the territory conquered by the Incas. On the day of the conjunction of the moon, at noon the Inca, with all the chiefs of his council, and the other principal lords who were in Cuzco, went to the Coricancha, which is the house and temple of the Sun, where they agreed together on the way in which the festival should be celebrated; for in one year they added, and in another they reduced the number of ceremonies, according to circumstances.

All things having been arranged, the High Priest addressed the assembly, and said that the ceremonies of the *Situa* should be performed, that the Creator might drive all the diseases and evils from the land. A great number of armed men, accoutred for war, with their lances, then came to the square in front of the temple. The figures called *Chuquilla* and *Uiracocha* were brought to the temple of the Sun from their own special temples....The priests of these huacas joined the assembly, and, with the concurrence of all present, the priest of the Sun proclaimed the feast. First, all strangers, all whose ears were broken, and all deformed persons were sent out of the city, it being said that they should take no part in the ceremony, because they were in that state as a punishment for some fault. Unfortunate people ought not to be present, it was believed, because their ill-luck might drive away some piece of good fortune. They also drove out the dogs, that they might not howl. Then the people, who were armed as if for war, went to the square of Cuzco, crying out: 'O sicknesses, disasters, misfortunes, and dangers, go forth from the land.' In the middle of the square, where stood the urn of gold which was like a fountain, that was used at the sacrifice of *chicha*, four hundred men of war assembled. One hundred faced towards Colla-suyu, which is the direction of the Sun-rising. One hundred faced to the westward, which is the direction of Chinchasuyu. Another hundred looked towards Antisuyu, which is the north, and the last hundred turned towards the south. They had with them all the arms that are used in their wars. As soon as those who came from the temple of the Sun arrived in the square, they cried out and said: 'Go forth all evils.' The people of Huvin-Cuzco carried these cries, and there they delivered them over to the mitimaes of Huayparya, who in their turn passed them to the mitimaes of Atahuaylla, and thus they were passed to the mitimaes of Huaray-pacha, who continued them as

Inca warriors exorcising evil spirits.

far as the river at Quiquisana, where they bathed themselves and their arms. Thus was the shouting ended in that direction....

Such was the ceremony for driving the sicknesses out of Cuzco. Their reason for bathing in these rivers was because they were rivers of great volume, and were supposed to empty themselves into the sea, and to carry the evils with them. When the ceremony commenced in Cuzco, all the people, great and small, came to their doors, crying out, shaking their mantles and *llicllas*, and shouting, 'Let the evils be gone. How greatly desired has this festival been by us. O creator of all things, permit us to reach another year, that we may see another feast like this.' They all danced, including the Inca, and in the morning twilight they went to the rivers and

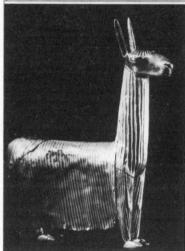

Funerary mask with inlays (top). Silver statuette used during rites to assure the fertility of llamas (above).

fountains to bathe, saying that their maladies would come out of them. Having finished bathing, they took great torches of straw, bound round with cords, which they lighted and continued to play with them, passing them from one to the other. They called these torches of straw *pancurcu*. At the end of their feast they returned to their houses, and by that time a pudding of coarsely ground maize had been prepared, called *sancu* and *elba*. This they applied to their faces, to the lintels of their doors, and to the places where they kept their food and clothes. Then they took the *sancu* to the fountains, and threw it in, saying, 'May we be free from sickness, and may no maladies enter this house.' They also sent this *sancu* to their relations and friends for the same purpose, and they put it on the bodies of their dead that they also might enjoy the benefits of the feast. Afterwards the women ate and drank their food with much enjoyment; and on this day each person, how poor soever he might be, was to eat and drink, for they said that on this day they should enjoy themselves, if they had to pass all the rest of the year in labour and sorrow. On this day no man scolded his neighbour, nor did any word pass in anger, nor did anyone claim what was owing to him from another. They said that there would be trouble and strife throughout the year, if any was commenced on the day of the festival.

In the night, the statues of the Sun, of the Creator, and of the Thunder, were brought out, and the priests of each of these statues warmed it with the before mentioned *sancu*. In the morning they brought the best food they could prepare to present at the temples of the Creator, of the Sun, and of the Thunder; which the priests of those *huacas* received and consumed. They also brought out the bodies of the dead lords and ladies which were embalmed, each one being brought out by the person of the same lineage who had charge of it. During the night these bodies were washed in the baths which belonged to them when they were alive. They were then brought back to their houses, and warmed with the same coarse pudding called *çancu* [sic]; and the food they had been most fond of when they were alive was placed before them, and afterwards the persons who were in charge of the bodies consumed the food.

The persons who had charge of the huaca called *Guana-caucique*, which is a great figure of a man, washed it and warmed it with the *sancu*; and the principal Inca lord and his wife, after

they had finished their bath, put the same *sancu* in their house, and on their hands. Afterwards, they placed certain plumes on their heads, of a bird called *pialco*, which are of a changing colour. The same was done with the figure of the Creator, and those who had charge of it called this ceremony *Pilcoyacu*. At about eight or nine in the morning the principal lord Inca, with his wife, and the lords of the council who were in his house, came forth into the great square of Cuzco, richly dressed. They also brought out the image of the Sun called *Apupunchau*, which was the principal image among those in the temple. They were accompanied by all the priests of the Sun, who brought the two figures of gold, and their women called Inca-Ollo and Palla-Ollo. There also came forth

Surrounded by members of the royal families, the Inca offers the sacred drink (maize beer), to his ancestor the Sun.

the woman called Coya-facssa, who was dedicated to the Sun. She was either the sister or the daughter of the ruler. The priests carried the image of the Sun, and placed it on a bench prepared for it in the square. The priests of the Creator likewise brought forth his image, and deposited it in its place. So also did the priests of the Thunder, called Chuqui-ylla, bring forth his image. Each had its bench of gold, and before them were borne *yauris*, which were made like sceptres of gold. The priests of these *huacas* came in very rich dresses, to celebrate this feast. Those who had charge of the *huaca* called Huanacauri, also brought its figure into the square. They say that a woman was never assigned to the *huaca* of the Creator. It was believed that the Creator did not need women, because, as he created them, they all belonged to him. In all their sacrifices, the first was offered to the Creator. At this feast they brought out all the embalmed bodies of their lords and ladies, very richly adorned. The bodies were carried by the descendants of the respective lineages, and were deposited in the square on seats of gold, according to the order in which they lived.

All the people of Cuzco came out, according to their tribes and lineages, as richly dressed as their means would allow; and, having made reverences to the Creator, the Sun, and the lord Inca, they sat down on their benches [and] passed the day in eating and drinking, and enjoying themselves; and they performed the *tauqui* called *alançitua saqui*, in red shirts down to their feet, and garlands called *pilco-casa* on their heads; accompanied with large or small tubes of canes, which made a kind of music called *tica-tica.* They gave thanks to the Creator for having spared them to

see that day, and prayed that they might pass another year without sickness; and they did the same to the Sun and to the Thunder. The Inca came with them, having the Sun before him. He had a great vase of gold containing chicha. It was received by the priest, who emptied it into the urn, which, as has been said, is like a stone fountain plated with gold. This urn had a hole made in such a way, that the chicha could enter a pipe or sewer passing under the ground to the houses of the Sun, the Thunder, and the Creator.

The next day they all came to the great square in the same order, placing the *huacas* on their benches as before. The Inca and the people brought with them a very great quantity of flocks.... The number of animals was so great, according to those who made this declaration, that they amounted to more than one hundred thousand, and it was necessary that all should be without spot or blemish, and with fleeces that had never been shorn. Presently the priest of the Sun selected four of the most perfect, and sacrificed them in the following order: one was offered to the Creator, another to the Thunder, another to the Sun, and another to Huanacauri. When this sacrifice was offered up, the priest had the *sancu* on great plates of gold, and he sprinkled it with the blood of the sheep. The high priest then said in a loud voice so that all might hear: 'Take heed how you eat this *sancu*; for he who eats it in sin, and with a double will and heart, is seen by our father, the Sun, who will punish him with grievous troubles. But he who with a single heart partakes of it, to him the Sun and the Thunder will show favour, and will grant children and happy years, and abundance, and all that he requires.' Then they all rose up to partake, first making a solemn vow before eating the *yahuar-sancu*, in which they promised never to murmur against the Creator, the Sun, or the Thunder; never to be traitors to their lord the Inca, on pain of receiving condemnation and trouble. The priest of the Sun then took what he could hold on three fingers, put it into his mouth, and returned to his seat. In this order, and in this manner of taking the oath, all the tribes rose up, and thus all partook down to the little children. They all kept some of the *yahuar-sancu* for those who were absent, and sent some to those who were confined to their beds by sickness; for they believed it to be very unlucky for any one not to partake of the *yahuar-sancu* on that day. They took it with such care that no particle was allowed to fall to the ground, this being looked upon as a great sin. When they killed the sacrificial sheep, they took out the lungs and inflated them, and the priests judged, from certain signs on them, whether all things would turn out prosperously in the coming year or not. Afterwards, they burnt them before the Creator, the Sun, and the Thunder. The bodies of the sheep were divided and distributed, as very sacred things, a very small piece to each person. The rest was given to the people of Cuzco to eat, and each man, as he entered the square, pulled off a piece of the wool, with which he sacrificed to the Sun.

Christobal de Molina
The Fables and Rites of the Incas, 1573
Translated by Clements R. Markham, 1873

Sacrifice of a black lamb on the day of Intiraymi, the great festival of the Sun.

'Archaeologist wants to reconquer shrine for Incas'

After the death of the last Inca, many traditional rites lost their relevance. And yet the Catholicism that developed in Peru was founded in more ways than one on the ancient Inca rituals.

CONƷEDERACION
COMOHIƷODIOSCIELO

The Christian god holds in his hands the deified heavenly bodies of the Incas.

The history of post-conquest Peru is in many ways typified by the struggles between the Catholic church and traditional Andean culture. Nowhere is this more apparent than at the monastery of Santo Domingo in Cuzco, where a colonial church sits atop one of the most important Inca buildings, the temple of the Sun. As this newspaper report reveals, archaeologists keen to investigate the Inca structure face serious opposition from the Catholic priests.

Cuzco, Peru – Raymundo Béjar Navarro, an archeologist, climbs the adobe wall up onto the grounds of the Santo Domingo monastery here in the center of town.

Shaking his head, he complains that the four resident monks are refusing to let his scientific team dig in the area. Defiantly, looking up at the towering, 350-year-old Spanish church, he hisses through his teeth, 'They should tear this down.'

The reason for such emotion is that the Santo Domingo church and monastery sit atop the holiest shrine of the Inca culture – the Temple of the Sun, or Koricancha [sic] in Quechua. And Mr Béjar is leading a three-year effort to restore the temple.

Two conflicting cultures

The church is indeed a mixture of the two conflicting cultures. Its foundations and supporting walls are of the exquisitely carved Inca stones, made out of andesite, that were carved with stone tools from quarries miles away, and so finely shaped at the building site that no mortar was needed. Even today, a knife does not fit between the joints.

Above the Inca masonry is the Spanish construction of roughly cut stones put together with adobe mortar, giving the

A fanciful reconstruction of the temple of the Sun at Cuzco.

church a two-tone texture. Inside, large parts of the guilded baroque monastery have been removed to reveal four stone chambers of the original Inca temple.

Recently the digging has produced a new phase of the centuries-old struggle between the conquerors and the conquered of Peru, between the modern-day Roman Catholic Church and the descendants of the Incas, who yielded to Francisco Pizarro in 1532.

'They have so many churches throughout Peru,' Mr Béjar said. 'Why do they have to have one right on top of the holiest Inca site? I thought this was the year when the church was apologizing for past abuses. If they abused anyone, they abused the Incas.'

Mr Béjar, who is a Roman Catholic, has beliefs that have not sat well with the church hierarchy. His thinking has been called blasphemy, and he has received threats of excommunication. Lawsuits have been filed by the Dominican

monastery against the city of Cuzco to prevent any 'robbing of church property'.

'The capricious Mr Béjar is pretending to take down a church that has been declared a world monument by Unesco,' said the Revd Domingo Gamarra, director of the monastery. 'The church represents the meeting of two cultures. What he is doing is anti-Christian, and we will defend the church to the very end.'

Until conquered by the Spanish, the Temple of the Sun was the center of the vast Inca empire that stretched from northern Venezuela to Patagonia in southern Argentina. Here was the repository of the realm's gold treasure, showcase of its exquisite stone carving technology and central seat of government.

As was customary when the Spaniards conquered an area, they imposed Catholicism on the Incas and used the

Koricancha structure as a church. In 1650 an earthquake destroyed part of the temple, so the Spanish tore most of the temple down and used the finely cut stones to build the existing church and monastery.

In 1953 another quake hit the building. Many of the Spanish-built walls collapsed, revealing parts of the original structure hidden for centuries. In reconstructing Santo Domingo, church officials agreed not to build on some of the existing Inca walls.

For Jesus Cheque, a Quechua Indian working on the digging project, the idea of the Santo Domingo church resting atop the Inca temple is a bitter one, and he says flatly that he wants the church torn down.

'It's the symbol of the oppression of our culture, the abuse of my Andean past,' he said. 'Where is my place to worship? They have stolen the stones of my temple.'

Such cultural sensitivities are being fed by politicians. Daniel Estrada, Mayor of Cuzco, in his third term, has been highly successful, appealing to the Inca roots of Cuzqueños, as Cuzco residents are known.

Mayor pledges sensitivity

'This is a victimized society, oppressed and suppressed for centuries, and we intend to change that by being sensitive to the Andean beliefs,' Mr Estrada said. 'For them Cuzco is the Sacred City.'

Recently, Mr Estrada has invested money earned from taxes on soft drinks and other items to rejuvenate Cuzco, installing fountains, rebuilding narrow streets in the old part of town and putting up a 40-foot statue of the great Inca emperor, Pachacútec, on top of a 110-foot stone base, at a cost of more than $1 million.

But Koricancha represents his most ambitious project. Using $2 million of the municipality's funds, the Mayor bought the land around the temple, tore down the existing houses and began excavating in the area that once was the outer court.

But motives to resurrect the Inca culture have a mercantile side as well. The Inca ruins around Cuzco, including the breathtaking Machu Picchu, have created Peru's tourist engine. But problems with guerrilla violence and cholera in early 1991 cut tourism down to 15 percent of its levels in the early 1980s. This has left 40 percent of Cuzqueños unemployed and 20 percent underemployed.

Slight recovery in tourism

Tourism has seen a slight recovery in the two and a half years since the outbreak of cholera in early 1991, but only to 40 percent of previous levels.

A restored Koricancha is considered to be a major piece in reviving tourism in Cuzco. But if the dispute is not resolved, it may look like just nondescript ruins next to a colonial church. And, what's more, the most scientifically important site of Koricancha – the central temple chamber – may never be touched by archeologists, since it rests directly under the church's sanctuary.

'The monks don't want to let anyone dig, because they are afraid they'll lose the property,' said Prof. John Rowe, an archeologist at the University of California in Berkeley and an adviser to the Koricancha project. 'They are only a few monks in a huge piece of property, but no one here wants to take on the church.'

Nathaniel C. Nash
The New York Times, 31 August 1993

The church of Santo Domingo, built on the foundations of Coricancha – the temple of the Sun at Cuzco.

When two worlds collide

The Spanish conquest brought about a veritable revolution in the New World: a demographic collapse due to the introduction of new diseases, a mingling of populations, and an ecological upheaval through the arrival of European animals and plants. Brutally, the Old World invaded the New.

The disease factor

The huge epidemics that wiped out nine-tenths of the Indian population is a factor that tends to be overlooked in the dramatic story of the conquest. But besides affecting the numerical strength of the native peoples, it struck lethally at the survivors' will to resist.

All these factors conspired to make Amerindian populations radically vulnerable to the disease organisms Spaniards and, before long, also Africans, brought with them across the ocean. The magnitude of the resultant disaster has only recently become clear. Learned opinion before World War II systematically underestimated Amerindian populations, putting the total somewhere between eight and fourteen million at the time Columbus landed in Hispaniola. Recent estimates, however, based on sampling of tribute lists, missionary reports and elaborate statistical arguments, have multiplied such earlier estimates tenfold and more, putting Amerindian population on the eve of the conquest at about one hundred million, with twenty-five to thirty million of this total assignable to the Mexican and an approximately equal number to the Andean civilizations. Relatively dense populations also apparently existed in the connecting Central American lands.

Starting from such levels, population decay was catastrophic. By 1568, less than fifty years from the time Cortez [sic] inaugurated epidemiological as well as other exchanges between Amerindians and European populations, the population of central Mexico had

Dance of the Blacks and mulattos of Lima.

shrunk to about three million, i.e., to about one tenth of what had been there when Cortez landed. Decay continued, though at a reduced rate, for another fifty years, reaching a low point of about 1.6 million by 1620. Recovery did not definitely set in for another thirty years or so and remained very slow until the eighteenth century.

Similarly drastic destruction of pre-existing Amerindian societies also occurred in other parts of the Americas, continuing even into the twentieth century. Disaster is to be expected whenever some previously remote and isolated tribe comes into contact with the outside world and there encounters a series of destructive and demoralizing epidemics. A relatively recent case history will illustrate how ruthless and seemingly irresistible such a process can be. In 1903 a South American tribe, the Cayapo, accepted a missionary – a single priest – who bent every effort to safeguard his flock from the evils and dangers of civilization. When he arrived the tribe was between six thousand and eight thousand strong, yet only five hundred survived in 1918. By 1927 only twenty-seven were alive and in 1950 two or three individuals tracing descent to the Cayapo still existed, but the tribe had totally disappeared – and this despite the best intentions and a deliberate attempt to shield the Indians from disease as well as other risks of outside contacts....

Clearly, if smallpox had not come when it did, the Spanish victory could not have been achieved in Mexico. The same was true of Pizarro's filibuster into Peru. For the smallpox epidemic in Mexico did not confine its ravages to Aztec territory. Instead, it spread to Guatemala, where it appeared in 1520, and continued southward, penetrating

B urial rites for an important member of the community.

the Inca domain in 1525 or 1526. Consequences there were just as dramatic as among the Aztecs. The reigning Inca died of the disease while away from his capital on campaign in the North. His designated heir also died, leaving no legitimate successor. Civil war ensued, and it was amid this wreckage of the Inca political structure that Pizarro and his crew of roughnecks made their way to Cuzco and plundered its treasures. He met no serious military resistance at all.

Two points seem particularly worth emphasizing here. First, Spaniards and Indians readily agreed that epidemic disease was a particularly dreadful and unambiguous form of divine punishment. Interpretation of pestilence as a sign of God's displeasure was a part of the Spanish inheritance, enshrined in the Old Testament and in the whole Christian tradition. The Amerindians, lacking all experience of anything remotely like the initial series of lethal epidemics, concurred. Their religious doctrines recognized that superhuman power lodged in deities whose behaviour towards men was often angry. It was natural, therefore, for them to assign an unexampled effect to a supernatural cause, quite apart from the Spanish missionary efforts that urged the same interpretation of the catastrophe upon dazed and demoralized converts.

Secondly, the Spaniards were nearly immune from the terrible disease that raged so mercilessly among the Indians. They had almost always been exposed in childhood and so developed effective immunity. Given the interpretation of the cause of pestilence accepted by both parties, such a manifestation of divine partiality for the invaders was conclusive. The gods of the Aztecs as much as the God of the Christians seemed to agree that the white newcomers had divine approval for all they did. And while God thus seemed to favour the whites, regardless of their morality and piety or lack thereof, his wrath was visited upon the Indians with an unrelenting harshness that often puzzled and distressed the Christian missionaries who soon took charge of the moral and religious life of their converts along the frontiers of Spain's American dominions.

From the Amerindian point of view, stunned acquiescence in Spanish superiority was the only possible response. No matter how few their numbers or how brutal and squalid their behaviour, the Spaniards prevailed. Native authority structures crumbled; the old gods seemed to have abdicated. The situation was ripe for the mass

conversions recorded so proudly by Christian missionaries. Docility to the commands of priests, viceroys, landowners, mining entrepreneurs, tax collectors, and anyone else who spoke with a loud voice and had a white skin was another inevitable consequence. When the divine and natural orders were both unambiguous in declaring against native tradition and belief, what ground for resistance remained? The extraordinary ease of Spanish conquests and the success a few hundred men had in securing control of vast areas and millions of persons is unintelligible on any other basis.

William H. McNeill
Plagues and Peoples, 1976

Pigmentocracy

The colonial and post-colonial history of the Andean region is dominated by the increasing racial mix of European, native American and Black. At first the Spaniards attempted to control this process, or at least to define it. But in the end all such efforts proved useless.

As mixing of races proceeded and the number of recognized mixtures increased, social ranking in Spanish America grew more complex and subtle. In the sixteenth century, colonial society divided broadly into Indians and Europeans. Blacks were in general associated with the European side, being regarded by both Indians and Europeans as servants and agents of the colonists. For several decades after the military conquests, pre-existing native social distinctions persisted to a surprising degree. But in the middle decades of the sixteenth century, with the rise of Spanish bureaucracy and a consequent and intentional reduction of the political role played up to then by local native rulers, native society suffered a downward levelling. At the same time, settler society began to acquire a more defined and permanent set of stratifications....

Between the extremes of controllers and conquered, ever-growing numbers of mixed-blooded people, neither one nor the other in historical identity, entered society in the middle colonial period. At first, standing was ascribed to them above all according to the degree of their physical resemblance to Europeans or Indians. *Mestizos* whose appearance was almost Spanish would find themselves regarded and treated almost as Spaniards. Conversely those who could barely be distinguished from Indians might find themselves counted as such, and in danger of having the Indians' obligations of tribute and draft labour thrust upon them. The more European a person's appearance, the wider became the range of economic opportunities generally available to him. Similarly, *pardos* of mixed blood who closely resembled Blacks might well find themselves being regarded and treated

very much as if slaves. This system of ascription of social standing existing in Spanish America after 1600 has sometimes been called a 'pigmentocracy'; and indeed, skin colour (or rather, the degree to which an individual's physical appearance approached the ideal of 'Whiteness', 'Indianness' or 'Blackness') does seem to have set status and put limits on that person's economic and social possibilities.

The gradations of colour and appearance produced by ethnic mixing sat well with the Spanish predilection, deriving from Catholic medieval sources, to view society as a natural hierarchy. Each member had his or her place and function in the structure, from which it was difficult, and even to some extent wrong, to move. Inequality, furthermore, was implicit in such a hierarchy. These conceptions were implanted in Spanish America in the sixteenth century and have persisted there to a greater or lesser degree to the present.

Nonetheless, there was a limit to which 'pigmentocracy' could ultimately serve the purposes of such a scheme. As

In the 18th century, an artist was commissioned to paint a series of pictures illustrating the racial hierarchy. (Left) A *mulatto*, the child of a Spaniard and a Black; and (right) a *morisco*, the child of a Spaniard and a *mulatta*.

the increase of mixed-blooded people accelerated in the seventeenth century and the number of combinations of Indian, Black and White grew, ever more discriminating descriptive terms were coined to categorize them. For example, the child of a Spaniard and *mulatto* was termed a *morisco* (Moor); that of a Spaniard and a *morisco*, an *albino*; that of an *albino* and a Spaniard, a *tornatrás* ('turn back'); that of a Spaniard and a *tornatrás, tente en el aire* ('stay up in the air'); and so on, through dozens of finely divided categories. But the practical difficulty was that given the variable workings of genetics, it was impossible to deduce someone's parenthood from his or her appearance with this degree of precision. The children of, say, a *mestizo* (a person of mixed Spanish and Indian blood) and a *mulatto* (a person of mixed Spanish and African blood) might range in appearance anywhere within the boundaries of pure Indian, pure Black, and pure White; and would probably differ significantly in pigment and features one from another. The attempt to form a precise hierarchy based on fine differences of genetic origin, as judged by appearance, was therefore doomed; and it seems, in fact, more of a rearguard neo-scholastic exercise than anything else. In practice, the quainter terms of genetic description were little, if ever, used. Most people came simply to be placed in the broad categories of Spaniard, *criollo*, Indian, Black, *mestizo* and *mulatto*.

Another change in the criteria of social ranking accompanied the inevitable decline of fine gradation measured by ethnic appearance. This was the increase of the importance of wealth as a determinant of rank. In truth, wealth had from the start probably been more

powerful in this respect than it was in Spain. After crossing the Atlantic (itself considered a feat admirable enough to bring a gain in status), immigrants, whether of high or low position in Spain, found the standing ascribed to them at home falling away, growing less confining, as if a skin were being shed. In comparison with Spain, then, the power of wealth, or of its lack, to modify social standing was increased in America. Similarly, once maintaining a social hierarchy according to ethnic appearance became problematical, an individual's wealth contributed more than before to defining his status. At the same time, however, ethnicity still had much to do with access to economic opportunity. Someone clearly Indian or Black was unlikely in the extreme to become a merchant operating in the intercontinental or intercolonial trade, or the owner of large silver mines, or of a large hacienda; whereas a *mestizo*, especially one distinctly European in appearance, might possibly aspire to such occupations. Much the same is still true today of those parts of modern Spanish America that have an Indian or Black component in their populations (as do all the major countries to a significant extent except Argentina, Chile and Uruguay). Wealth, if he can get it, may carry a person up the social scale; but getting it may be an insuperable problem in the first place.

Peter Bakewell
From *The Hispanic World*
Ed. J. H. Elliott, 1991

The olive, the Mediterranean tree par excellence, was not planted in the Spanish-American colonies because Spain wanted to keep its commercial monopoly in olive oil.

Many places in this kingdom, such as the coast valleys and the land on the banks of rivers, are very fertile, and yield wheat, maize, and barley in great quantities. There are also not a few vineyards at San Miguel, Truxillo, the City of the Kings, Cuzco, and Guamanga, and they are beginning to plant them in other parts, so that there is great hope of profitable vine cultivation. There are orange and pomegranate trees, and other trees brought from Spain, besides those of the country; and pulses of all sorts.

In short, Peru is a grand country, and hereafter it will be still greater, for large cities have been founded, and when our age has passed away, Peru may send to other countries, wheat, meat, wool, and even silk, for there are the best situations in the world for planting mulberries. There is only one thing that has not yet been brought to this country, and that is the olive tree, which, after bread and the vine, is the most important product. It seems to me that if young plants were brought from Spain, and planted in the coast valleys, and on the banks of rivers in the mountains, there would soon be as large olive woods as there are at Axarafe de Sevilla. For if they require a warm climate it is here; if they want much water, or none, or little, all these requirements can be found here. In some places in Peru it never thunders, lightning is not seen, nor do snows fall in the coast valleys, and these are the things which damage the fruit of olive trees. When the trees are once planted, there will soon come a time when Peru

Harvesting maize in the month of May. Imperfect cobs were used for making *chicha* beer.

will be as well supplied with oil as with everything else. No woods of oak trees have been found in Peru, but if they were planted in the Collao, in the district of Cuzco, and in other parts, I believe that they would give the same result as olive trees in the coast valleys.

My opinion is that the conquerors and settlers of these parts should not pass their time in fighting battles and matching in chase of each other; but in planting and sowing, which would be much more profitable.

Pedro Cieza de León
Chronicle of Peru, 1553
Translated by Clements R. Markham, 1864

I n the 19th century, Peruvian exoticism took on very strange forms, like this Andean woman dressed in Moorish fashion.

Inca tribute

Colonial tribute was inspired by the Inca system of tribute, and took it as its model in every way, while failing to take into consideration the ideology of reciprocity that had legitimized it.

Money played no part in the Inca economy. Nevertheless goods circulated throughout the Empire, albeit in a somewhat limited fashion: in the first place by barter, but above all through the tribute system.

As we have seen, crops varied with altitude and mountain farmers exchanged their produce for that of the lower valleys: we know that a system of complementary production from high and low lands was the basis of a 'vertical economy'. Thus the people of Chucuito, on Lake Titicaca, bartered llama wool, *charqui* and *chuño* for maize from the Sama and Moquega regions on the coast, and for the coca from Larecaja and Capinota, in the tropical valleys of the interior. In these transactions, considerable distances were covered.

More generally, the circulation of goods throughout the Empire was ensured by the tribute paid to the Inca: either produce from the Inca's lands came directly to Cuzco or the Inca transferred from one region to another goods that had accumulated in his storehouses. But it was a relatively limited circulation; for one thing we must reckon on considerable local consumption; for another, the peasants owed tribute not only to the Inca, but also to the whole hierarchy of the *curacas*.

All males in the communities between the ages of 25 and 50 (and under 25 if married) were taxpayers, i.e. tributaries (*hatunruna*). Essentially the peasants owed their labour, not the produce of the *ayllu* territory. (But the two were linked: according to the principle of reciprocity, obligation to pay tribute was associated with the right to a share of communal land.) All the *curacas,* from the governor of a province to the chieftain of 100 men, were exempt from manual work and therefore from tribute. There was however one special category of tributaries: the artisans. These men (potters, goldsmiths etc.) owed only the products of their own craft and were free of all other obligations.

Labourers construct the boundaries of the empire.

Tribute paid to the Inca was paralleled by tribute paid to the *curaca*. In practice, the peasants' obligations were of the following three types:

A. *Collective work on the land.* The fields of the Inca and of the *curacas* were productive only if their owners had a work-force at their disposal. This was supplied in the first instance by the whole of the community: *ayllu* members went off together to the Inca's land to tend it communally. Their work was done to the rhythm of songs and dances of a religious character and the occasion had its place in a total integrated view of the world. The same applied to the *curacas'* land. Thus ties of solidarity among members of the *ayllu* were put at the service of the State and of its administrative apparatus. Produce from the Inca's fields was stored in local or

I n each village, the women wove in order to
  pay tribute.

provincial storehouses. It appears that
the *curacas*, or at any rate the more
important of them, also had their own
storehouses.

B. *Mita*, personal, periodic service.
For the army, or for large-scale projects
(the building of roads, bridges, temples,
etc.) the State recruited a certain number
of tributaries according to requirements
and for limited periods of time. *Ayllu*
members, conforming to the rules of
solidarity, tilled the fields of the absent
tributaries. The great projects organized
by the State excited the admiration of
the chroniclers, and historians have long
insisted on the importance of the *mita*
performed for the Incas. But the *curacas*

could also draw on this form of tribute,
whether for their domestic needs or for
the cultivation of their fields or the
guarding of their herds. Thus at
Chucuito, Martín Cari had sixty Indians
working for him every year and Martín
Cusi had thirty. And as in the case of
community work, the *mitayos* were both
fed and rewarded by Inca or *curaca*.

C. *Textile tribute.* Woven fabrics and
clothes played a special role in the Inca
State: J.V. Murra has shown that they
had not only economic but also religious
and magical significance; they were
burnt or buried in sacrifices to the
huacas and to the gods. When the
Spanish arrived, they were astonished at
the vast stores of cloth contained in the
State depots. In fact every family spun
and wove for the Inca its own quota of
tribute, which varied with the supplies
available. But it is always made clear that
the Inca expected to draw on the
communal store; here again they owed
their labour, no more. For example in
the Huánuco region, in the north of the
Empire, herds of llamas were few and
the farmers grew cotton: but according
to the informants of Ortiz de Zúñiga,
the communities owed woolen fabrics as
tribute, the wool itself being provided by
the Inca. The same arrangement
operated between peasants and *curacas*:
the latter also levied tribute of woven
fabrics, providing the raw material
themselves. One may wonder whether
this tribute was a tax on the whole of the
community or only on the *mitayos* doing
their annual service for the *curaca*. From
what we know of Martín Cari it seems
that both possibilities existed.

In short, tribute was an integral part
of the system of reciprocity: the peasants
tilled the Inca's land in exchange for the
right to use community land: similarly,
in exchange for the right to draw on the

community's wool (or cotton) they wove the Inca's wool. These obligations did not result solely from notions of the universal proprietorial rights of the Inca: he, the son of the Sun, was the source of divine protection for his subjects, he assured the order of society and bestowed favours and rewards. In particular, the Inca's generosity provided for the welfare of those who were old or sick and unable to work. In time of famine, he distributed to the communities the reserve stocks from his granaries. The peasants felt therefore that they shared in the consumption of the produce they delivered as tribute. The *curaca* played a similar role lower down the scale. In fact, duties to the Inca seem to have been an extension of duties to the *curaca*, as though the Empire had established itself by modelling its institutions on those already in existence. In conclusion, it amounted to a dual system of gifts and counter-gifts as shown in the diagram:

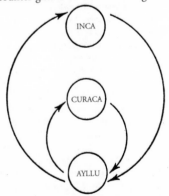

This dual system then consisted of central collection of goods by the Inca and their subsequent redistribution to the Empire.... However, despite the Inca's role, tribute was mainly a local

matter. We must not overlook the importance of provincial administration: the greater part of stocks was consumed locally and most of the *mitayos* also served locally. We can therefore understand why the Inca forbade his subjects to leave their communities, except with his express permission: tribute weighed collectively on each *ayllu*, it was levied under the supervision of the *curacas* and consequently required a stable tribute-paying population. Hence a remarkable dialectical process: to some extent tribute enabled goods to circulate throughout the empire, but at the same time it reinforced social immobility. For one thing, the communal system itself assumed a degree of stability: it was founded on patterns of kinship, on the redistribution of land, and the *ayllu* member could scarcely imagine himself breaking the ties of reciprocity which were for him the definition of social life. For another, rotation of the *mita*, collective work on the Inca's land, situated irrevocably in their own territory, bound the tributaries to the *ayllu* of their birth. In conclusion, tribute played a double role: it linked the community to a much greater unit, but at the same time it isolated it in its local setting and consolidated its traditional structures.

Colonial tribute

The basic problem is: how did the Spanish tribute compare with the Inca tribute? Quantitatively, we lack precise data. However, at Huánuco, Chucuito and Huaura we have witnessed a development of grave consequence: the Spanish appropriated lands belonging to the Inca and the Sun, lands formerly reserved for tribute; as a result, the burden of tribute was transferred to the

V iew of Chulumani (top), capital of the province of Yungas in Bolivia. Above: a Chorrillos man in festival outfit (Peru).

communal lands of the Indian people. Often the tax codes themselves, under Gasca as under Toledo, explicitly confirm that the tributaries were to harvest their tribute of maize and wheat from their own fields. It is true that the Indians were less numerous and in general...were not short of land (although they had lost the best); but precisely because they were fewer in number, they had more work to do. It is therefore not surprising that Spanish tribute seemed to them much more burdensome than that of the Inca: the indications we have concerning the amount of time spent in working to pay the *encomenderos'* dues (at Huánuco and at Huaura) seem to point to an intensive exploitation of the Indian population. It would be naive to assume that the tax beneficiaries obeyed the laws to the letter: innumerable documents bear witness to malpractices, illicit levies and violence. We know that an unscrupulous despot ruled at Huaura. Returning to the Huánuco region, we may recall the case of Sebastián Núñez de Prado. For nine years this man exacted 300 baskets of coca per annum instead of the prescribed 80. And to levy the textile tribute, he imprisoned a certain number of Indians in a corral where they were forced to work without respite. As for his neighbour, García Ortiz de Espinosa, he was ordered to make restitution of 1000 pesos to his tributaries, and was even jailed for ill-treating his Indians. But malpractices of the *encomenderos* were rarely punished.

Above all, there was a qualitative change: the ideology which had justified the Inca system lay in ruins: in a society dominated by the Spanish, notions of reciprocity and redistribution had become meaningless. Or, more exactly, the Spanish system made use of fragments of the former system; reciprocity still played a part in the relations between *ayllus* and *curacas* and the latter still acted as intermediaries between the Indians and their new masters; but while reciprocity had maintained a rotation of wealth (even though fictitious or unequal) between *ayllu*, *curaca* and Inca, Spanish rule brought about a one-way transfer of goods from Indians to Spaniards, without return. Let us remember a few significant facts: at Huaura the tributaries received neither food nor tools for their work; at Huánuco, the Chupacho Indians unanimously complained that they were obliged to provide cotton for the textile tribute; at Chucuito, whereas the *curaca* still provided wool for his Indians when they wove cloth for him, the King did nothing of the kind for the thousand pieces of *ropa* he received; and the 18,000 pesos paid to His Majesty did not return in any form whatever to the Indians. The Spanish ruler had taken the place of the Inca, he had inherited his

centralizing role, but he no longer ensured redistribution of wealth for the benefit of all. In conclusion, whereas Inca tribute had functioned as a balanced and circular economic structure, Spanish tribute was chiefly remarkable for its unbalanced, unilateral structure.

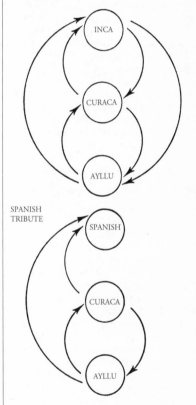

INCA TRIBUTE

SPANISH TRIBUTE

Nathan Wachtel
The Vision of the Vanquished, 1971
Translated by Ben and Siân Reynolds, 1977

Martín Llapa's complaint against Don Francisco Fernández

This document of 1750 is one of the very numerous complaints lodged by the Indians with the competent tribunals to protest at abuses by the Spanish or mixed - race landowners.

Martín Llapa, a native Indian from the place known as Los Azogues, subject of Don Matias Tenempaguay, principal cacique of the Indians of the subject faction called Mageo in the said village....I declare that Don Francisco Fernández, a neighbour in the said town, without the slightest title or right to an allocation of Indians to serve in his hacienda, Tarque, and without my having been designated by my above-mentioned cacique, by his own authority and powerful hand, inopportunely seized me in my house and, with the worst disgrace, harshness and tyranny, took me to his aforesaid hacienda, telling me that he had the authority to force me to serve him for as many years as he wished, and he did so, and promptly put me in charge of a flock of sheep without giving me a chance to put my poor house in order or the little sowed crops I had which were now ripe, or to gather my fruits, and all this was lost because of him, and it is now my due to recuperate this without the slightest difficulty, and being an ignorant and timid Indian, and believing that my cacique had designated me for service, I obeyed him and humbled myself to serve him for a year and two months, unjustly, because I had not been so designated at all, so that he had committed an offence against my cacique by usurping his right, and an offence against me by making me work without the slightest reward, because he

The burden of Spanish labour: an Inca girl is forced to spin, herd and carry wood at the same time.

did not even give me the third of a full year's tribute, a sum which I owe the collector, and which necessarily has to be paid by him for having caused the debt while I was working for him, and even less did he give me monthly wages, because the first month he only gave me two and a half fanegas of barley, and through the whole year and two months there was no other reward than what I have just declared, and although I asked him for assistance he refused harshly. What's more, he did not even give me the cape that was mine by right, saying that the allocated Indian servant could ask for neither wages nor clothing, and seeing that the situation was one of resistance and destitution, I survived this whole period by borrowing wages from several Indians, not without difficulty, and I am now indebted to them as well, because my house was more than a day's walk away, which did not make my survival any easier; on top of all this there were greater wrongs, such as when Don Francisco had entrusted me with the flock, he warned his major-domo to send me out every day to labour, sow and weed and do the other usual tasks of the hacienda, without giving me the slightest salary, whereas this kind of work ought to have a different wage, and if by chance I refused I was immediately punished with beatings and floggings, and because of this the whole year went by with me serving in the fields, and I left my poor wife in charge of the flock, though she also had to carry out her personal chores, as was proper, and she was also set to the task of spinning wool and cotton fibres by Doña Petrona Abad, legitimate wife of the afore-mentioned Don Francisco Fernández, saying that as mistress of the house she had the power and authority to make her spin everything she gave her, and if she did not hand in the finished work within eight days, the major-domo was ordered to collect the work, and, if it was unfinished, to punish her, an order which the aforesaid major-domo carried out with the greatest cruelty, beating and flogging her, and seeing how we were so exhausted by this kind of work and such inhuman treatment, which is not meted out anywhere else in the world to wretched Indians, I withdrew from the said hacienda and rushed to my aforementioned cacique to tell him of the tasks which my wife and I had suffered because of him....And I learned that the said Don Francisco, in revenge for my fleeing his hacienda, is lodging unjust accusations about loss of sheep, in order to make me a slave to his service, because even if it were true that a few sheep were missing, I am under no obligation to pay him the slightest *real* if my work and that of my wife has not first been paid for, considering the fact that I spent more time labouring in the fields, and when Indians guard livestock they must not be occupied with anything else if they are to be held responsible for eventual losses, and although the aforesaid flock was entrusted to my wife, she, having to do spinning chores as well, could not pasture them freely but rather exposed to danger, since she did not even have a son to help her, and in order to make me pay he has taken my poor elderly mother, and I am assured he is keeping her prisoner in the said hacienda, without informing any judge....

Translated from the original text, Quito National Historical Archives, Indigenous Section

The colonial authorities built the town of Guanuco using a native workforce.

In search of the ancient Incas

One of the earliest archaeological studies of the Andes was conducted in the second half of the 19th century by the American Ephraim George Squier. Trained as a surveyor, Squier carried out detailed investigations of the ancient ruins and produced accurate plans and measurements. In this extract from his travelogue he follows an ancient Inca roadway.

Portrait of Squier.

Between Cuzco and the sweet valley of Yucay, there are numerous traces of an ancient road, some sections of which are perfect. These sections coincide in character with the long reaches in the direction of Quito. They consist of a pathway from ten to twelve feet [3.5–4 metres] wide, raised slightly in the centre, paved with stones, and the edges defined by lines of larger stones sunk firmly in the ground. Where this road descends from the elevated *puna* – a sheer descent of almost four thousand feet into the valley of Yucay – it zigzags on a narrow shelf cut in the face of the declivity, and supported here and there, where foothold could not otherwise be obtained, by high retaining-walls of cut stone, looking as perfect and firm as when first built centuries ago.

High mountain-ranges and broad and frigid deserts, swept by fierce, cold winds, are not the sole obstacles to intercommunication in the Altos of Peru, and among those snow-crowned monarchs of the Andes and Cordilleras. There are deep valleys, gorges, and ravines among these mountains, or cut deep in the plains that alternate with them, in which flow swelling rivers or rapid torrents, fed by the melting snows in the dry season, and swollen by the rains in the wet season. They are often unfordable; but still they must somehow be passed by the traveller. A few bridges of stone were constructed by the Spaniards, some after the Conquest; but, as a rule, the rivers and mountain torrents are passed to-day by the aid of devices the same as were resorted to by the Incas, and at points which they selected. Had the principle of the arch been well understood by the ancient inhabitants, who have left some of the finest stone-cutting and masonry to be found in the world, there is no doubt the interior of Peru would have abounded in bridges rivalling those of Rome in extent and beauty. As it was, occupying a country destitute of timber, they resorted to suspension bridges, no doubt precisely like those now constructed by their descendants and successors – bridges formed of cables of braided withes, stretched from bank to bank, and called *puentes de mimbres* (bridges of withes). Where the banks are high, or where the streams are compressed between steep or precipitous rocks, these cables are anchored to piers of stone. In other places they are approached by inclined causeways, raised to give them the necessary elevation above the water. Three or four cables form the floor and the principal support of the bridge, over which small sticks, sometimes only sections of cane or bamboo, are laid transversely, and fastened to the cables by vines, cords, or thongs of raw hide. Two smaller cables are sometimes stretched on each side, as a guard or hand-rail. Over these frail and swaying structures pass men and animals, the latter frequently with their loads on their backs....

The Apurimac is one of the head-waters of the Amazon, a large and rapid stream, flowing in a deep valley, or, rather, gigantic ravine, shut in by high and precipitous mountains. Throughout its length it is crossed at only a single point, between two enormous cliffs, which rise dizzily on both sides, and from the summits of which the traveller looks down into a dark gulf. At the bottom gleams a white line of water, whence struggles up a dull but heavy roar, giving to the river its name, *Apu-rimac*, signifying, in the Quichua [sic] tongue, 'the great speaker'. From above, the bridge, looking like a mere thread, is reached by a path which on

Engraving of the bridge over the Apurimac from Squier's book.

one side traces a thin, white line on the face of the mountain, and down which the boldest traveller may hesitate to venture....It is usual for the traveller to time his day's journey so as to reach this bridge in the morning, before the strong wind sets in; for, during the greater part of the day, it sweeps up the cañon of the Apurimac with great force, and then the bridge sways like a gigantic hammock, and crossing is next to impossible.

Ephraim George Squier
Peru: Incidents of Travel and Exploration in the Land of the Incas, 1877

The discovery of Machu Picchu

Rather than a professional archaeologist, Hiram Bingham was passionately interested in all the curiosities of South America. Knowing the texts of the early chroniclers, he drew on their narratives to reach the 'lost city', thus giving historical reality to a site which, until then, had lived only in legend.

We passed an ill-kept, grass-thatched hut, turned off the road through a tiny clearing, and made our camp at the edge of the river on a sandy beach. Opposite us, beyond the huge granite boulders which interfered with the progress of the surging stream, the steep mountain was clothed with thick jungle. Since we were near the road yet protected from the curiosity of passers-by, it seemed to be an ideal spot for a camp. Our actions, however, aroused the suspicions of the owner of the hut, Melchor Arteaga, who leased the lands of Mandor Pampa. He was anxious to know why we did not stay at his 'tavern' like other respectable travellers. Fortunately the Prefect of Cuzco, our old friend J.J. Nuñez, had given us an armed escort who spoke Quichua. Our gendarme, Sergeant Carrasco, was able to reassure the innkeeper. They had quite a long conversation. When Arteaga learned that we were interested in the architectural remains of the Incas, and were looking for the palace of the last Inca, he said there were some very good ruins in this vicinity – in fact, some excellent ones on top of the opposite mountain, called Huayna Picchu, and also on a ridge called Machu Picchu.

The morning of July 24th dawned in a cold drizzle. Arteaga shivered and seemed inclined to stay in his hut. I offered to pay him well if he would show me the ruins. He demurred and said it was too hard a climb for such a wet day. But when he found that I was willing to pay him a *sol* (a Peruvian silver dollar, 50 cents, gold), three or four times the ordinary daily wage in this vicinity, he finally agreed to go. When asked just

The temple of the Three Windows, at Machu Picchu.

T he expedition follows the gorges of the Urubamba.

where the ruins were, he pointed straight to the top of the mountain. No one supposed that they would be particularly interesting. And no one cared to go with me. Our naturalist said there were 'more butterflies near the river!' and he was reasonably certain he could collect some new varieties. Our surgeon said he had to wash his clothes and mend them. Anyhow it was my job to investigate all reports of ruins and try to find the Inca capital.

So, accompanied only by Sergeant Carrasco, I left camp at ten o'clock. Arteaga took us some distance upstream. On the road we passed a snake which had only just been killed. He said the region was the favourite haunt of 'vipers'....

After a walk of three quarters of an hour Arteaga left the main road and plunged down through the jungle to the bank of the river. Here there was a primitive bridge which crossed the roaring rapids at its narrowest part, where the stream was forced to flow between two great boulders. The 'bridge' was made of half a dozen very slender logs, some of which were not long enough to span the distance between the boulders, but had been spliced and lashed together with vines!

Arteaga and the sergeant took off their shoes and crept gingerly across....It was obvious that no one could live for an instant in the icy cold rapids, but would immediately be dashed to pieces against the rocks. I frankly confess that I got down on my hands and knees and crawled across, 6 inches at a time. Even after we reached the other side I could not help wondering what would happen to the bridge if a particularly heavy shower should fall in the valley above. A light rain had fallen during the night and the river had risen so that the bridge was already threatened by the foaming rapids. It would not take much more to wash it away entirely. If this should happen during the day it might be very awkward. As a matter of fact, it did happen a few days later and when the next visitors attempted to cross the river at this point they found only one slender log remaining.

Leaving the stream, we now struggled up the bank through dense jungle, and in a few minutes reached the bottom of a very precipitous slope. For an hour and twenty minutes we had a hard climb. A good part of the distance we went on all fours, sometimes holding on by our fingernails. Here and there, a primitive ladder made from the roughly notched trunk of a small tree was placed in such a

Houses and surrounding walls of Machu Picchu (above and opposite).

way as to help one over what might otherwise have proved to be an impassable cliff. In another place the slope was covered with slippery grass where it was hard to find either handholds or footholds. Arteaga groaned and said that there were lots of snakes here. Sergeant Carrasco said nothing but was glad he had good military shoes....

Shortly after noon, just as we were completely exhausted, we reached a little grass-covered hut 2000 feet above the river where several good-natured Indians, pleasantly surprised at our unexpected arrival, welcomed us with dripping gourds full of cool, delicious water. Then they set before us a few cooked sweet potatoes. It seems that two Indian farmers, Richarte and Alvarez, had recently chosen this eagles' nest for their home. They said they had found plenty of terraces here on which to grow their crops. Laughingly they admitted they enjoyed being free from undesirable visitors, officials looking for army 'volunteers' or collecting taxes.

Richarte told us that they had been living here for years. It seems probable that, owing to its inaccessibility, the canyon has been unoccupied for several centuries, but with the completion of the new government road, settlers began once more to occupy this region....

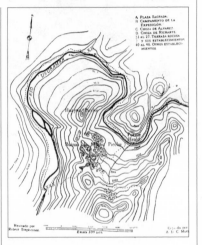

First topographic survey of the site of Machu Picchu, made by Bingham in 1912.

They said there were two paths to the outside world. Of one we had already had a taste; the other was 'even more difficult', a perilous path down the face of a rocky precipice on the other side of the ridge. It was their only means of egress in the wet season when the primitive bridge over which we had come could not be maintained. I was not surprised to learn that they went

away from home 'only about once a month'.

Through Sergeant Carrasco I learned that the ruins were 'a little further along'. In this country one never can tell whether such a report is worthy of credence. 'He may have been lying' is a good footnote to affix to all hearsay evidence. Accordingly, I was not unduly excited, nor in a great hurry to move. The heat was still great, the water from the Indians' spring was cool and delicious, and the rustic wooden bench, hospitably covered immediately after my arrival with a soft woollen *poncho*, most comfortable. Furthermore, the view was simply enchanting. Tremendous green precipices fell away to the white rapids of the Urubamba below. Immediately in front, on the north side of the valley, was a great granite cliff rising 2000 feet sheer. To the left was the solitary peak of Huayna Picchu, surrounded by seemingly inaccessible precipices. On all sides were rocky cliffs. Beyond them cloud-capped, snow-covered mountains rose thousands of feet above us.

We continued to enjoy the wonderful view of the canyon, but all the ruins we could see from our cool shelter were a few terraces.

Without the slightest expectation of finding anything more interesting than the ruins of two or three stone houses such as we had encountered at various places on the road between Ollantaytambo and Torontoy, I finally left the cool shade of the pleasant little hut and climbed further up the ridge and round a slight promontory. Melchor Arteaga had 'been there once before', so he decided to rest and gossip with Richarte and Alvarez. They sent a small boy with me as a 'guide'. The sergeant was in duty bound to follow, but I think he may have been a little curious to see what there was to see.

Hardly had we left the hut and rounded the promontory than we were confronted with an unexpected sight, a great flight of beautifully constructed stone-faced terraces, perhaps a hundred of them, each hundreds of feet long and 10 feet high. They had been recently rescued from the jungle by the Indians. A veritable forest of large trees which had been growing on them for centuries had been chopped down and partly burned to make a clearing for agricultural purposes. The task was too great for the two Indians so the tree trunks had been allowed to lie as they fell and only the smaller branches removed. But the ancient soil, carefully put in place by the Incas, was still capable of producing rich crops of maize and potatoes.

However, there was nothing to be excited about. Similar flights of well-made terraces are to be seen in the upper Urubamba Valley at Pisac and Ollantaytambo, as well as opposite

Torontoy. So we patiently followed the little guide along one of the widest terraces, where there had once been a small conduit, and made our way into an untouched forest beyond. Suddenly I found myself confronted with the walls of ruined houses built of the finest quality of Inca stone work. It was hard to see them for they were partly covered with trees and moss, the growth of centuries, but in the dense shadow, hiding in bamboo thickets and tangled vines, appeared here and there walls of white granite ashlars carefully cut and exquisitely fitted together. We scrambled along through the dense undergrowth, climbing over terrace walls and in bamboo thickets, where our guide found it easier going than I did. Suddenly, without any warning, under a huge overhanging ledge the boy showed me a cave beautifully lined with the finest cut stone. It had evidently been a royal mausoleum. On top of this particular ledge was a semi-circular building whose outer wall, gently sloping and slightly curved, bore a striking resemblance to the famous Temple of the Sun in Cuzco. This might also be a temple of the sun. It followed the natural curvature of the rock and was keyed to it by one of the finest examples of masonry I had ever seen. Furthermore it was tied into another beautiful wall, made of very carefully matched ashlars of pure white granite, especially selected for its fine grain. Clearly, it was the work of a master artist. The interior surface of the wall was broken by niches and square stone-pegs. The exterior surface was perfectly simple and unadorned. The lower courses, of particularly large ashlars, gave it a look of solidity. The upper courses, diminishing in size towards the top, lent grace and delicacy to the structure. The flowing lines, the

Royal tomb behind the temple of the Sun.

symmetrical arrangement of the ashlars, and the gradual gradation of the courses, combined to produce a wonderful effect, softer and more pleasing than that of the marble temples of the Old World. Owing to the absence of mortar, there were no ugly spaces between the rocks. They might have grown together. On account of the beauty of the white granite this structure surpassed in attractiveness the best Inca walls in Cuzco, which had caused visitors to marvel for four centuries. It seemed like an unbelievable dream. Dimly, I began to realize that this wall and its adjoining semicircular temple over the cave were as fine as the finest stonework in the world.

It fairly took my breath away. What could this place be? Why had no one given us any idea of it? Even Melchor Arteaga was only moderately interested and had no appreciation of the importance of the ruins which Richarte and Alvarez had adopted for their little farm. Perhaps after all this was an isolated small place which had escaped notice because it was inaccessible.

Then the little boy urged us to climb up a steep hill over what seemed to be a flight of stone steps. Surprise followed surprise in bewildering succession. We came to a great stairway of large granite blocks. Then we walked along a path to a clearing where the Indians had planted a small vegetable garden. Suddenly we found ourselves standing in front of the ruins of two of the finest and most interesting structures in ancient America. Made of beautiful white granite, the walls contained blocks of Cyclopean size, higher than a man. The sight had me spellbound.

Each building had only three walls and was entirely open on one side. The principal temple had walls 12 feet high which were lined with exquisitely made niches, five high up at each end, and seven on the back. There were seven courses of ashlars in the end walls. Under the seven rear niches was a rectangular block 14 feet long, possibly a sacrificial altar, but more probably a throne for the mummies of departed Incas, brought out to be worshipped. The building did not look as though it had ever had a roof. The top course of beautifully smooth ashlars was left uncovered so that the sun could be welcomed here by priests and mummies. I could scarcely believe my senses as I examined the larger blocks in the lower course and estimated that they must weigh from ten to fifteen tons each. Would anyone believe what I had found? Fortunately, in this land where accuracy in reporting what one has seen is not a prevailing characteristic of travellers, I had a good camera and the sun was shining.

The principal temple faces the south where there is a small plaza or courtyard. On the east side of the plaza was another amazing structure, the ruins of a temple containing three great windows looking out over the canyon to the rising sun. Like its neighbour, it is unique among Inca ruins. Nothing just like them in design and execution has ever been found. Its three conspicuously large windows, obviously too large to serve any useful purpose, were most beautifully made with the greatest care and solidity. This was clearly a ceremonial edifice of peculiar significance. Nowhere else in Peru, so far as I know, is there a similar structure conspicuous for being 'a masonry wall with three windows'. It will be remembered that Salcamayhua, the Peruvian who wrote an account of the antiquities of Peru in 1620, said that the first Inca, Manco the Great, ordered 'works to be executed at the place of his birth, consisting of a masonry wall with three windows'. Was that what I had found? If it was, then this was not the capital of the last Inca, but the birthplace of the first. It did not occur to me that it might be both. To be sure the region was one which could fit in with the requirements of Tampu-tocco, the place of refuge of the civilized folk who fled from the southern barbarian tribes after the battle of La Raya and brought with them the body of their king Pachacuti VI who was slain by an arrow. He might have been buried in the stone-lined cave under the semi-circular temple.

Hiram Bingham
Lost City of the Incas, 1951

The mysteries of Nazca

Limited to three valleys – those of Nazca, Ica and Pisco – on the southern coast of Peru, the Nazca culture, which reached its zenith between 350 BC and AD 650, has a primary place in the history of pre-Inca peoples. Although known for its ceramics, Nazca is most famous for its geoglyphs: immense drawings traced on the plains which still raise all kinds of questions.

Since the south coast, especially the valley of the Rio Grande de Nasca, is very arid, farmers clearly had to invent various methods for measuring time with the greatest precision possible, in order to master agricultural production, with its different phases of sowing, harvesting, preparing the soils and irrigation. In sites of the Nazca culture, archaeologists have noted the presence of agricultural terraces (indisputably a sign of careful treatment of the soil), of irrigation canals, and, apparently, of a few small dams or weirs. But the most remarkable feature is the organization of an extremely complex calendar, based on the tracing of an immense network of 'tracks' or drawings on the pampas of Ingenio, north of Cahuachi. This network, combining lines and other tracings of an astronomical nature with tracks and ritual or ceremonial figures, has disconcerted numerous travellers and observers who have been intrigued by the apparently mysterious aspect of these gigantic depictions on the desert pampas.

One of the strangest aspects of the Nazca lines and figures is that, because of their size, they can only be observed from above. All that can be seen from the ground are long lines that disappear on the horizon, whereas from a plane or helicopter one can grasp their full extent and shape. These tracings have given rise to the most fantastic hypotheses and explanations, including the idea – very fashionable today and highly exploited commercially – that they were made by extraterrestrials.... This fiction, created by certain authors with an excessive imagination and a gift for popular

Ceramic drum found at Nazca.

Geoglyph known as 'the whale' on the plains of Nazca.

writing, has succeeded in convincing many readers. All these speculations rest on the fact that the lines can only be seen from the sky, and consequently they could only have been traced by beings who had the means to fly, which clearly was not the case for the ancient Peruvians. But in fact, neither the zoomorphic representations and drawings nor the tracks and lines were made to be seen from the sky, but rather to be used on the ground. Moreover, the tracks are associated with remains of different phases of the Nazca culture, and one even finds lines superimposed on each other, which shows that they were made by men unaware that they were drawing on old tracings. Next to these lines one often finds fragments of pottery, piles of stones and even refuse indicating that they were used by the Nazca people. Finally, this type of tracing exists not only at Nazca but also in other parts of the Peruvian desert. In most cases, they fulfil an astronomical function, or serve as a calendrical system, but they have also been used as tracks, roads or signals for travellers: at Paracas, facing the bay, there is a giant cactus drawn on the side of a hill; it clearly constituted a kind of beacon for navigators; the fishermen of the region call it the Candelabra.

According to the studies of Gerald Hawkins and determinations by John Rowe and Dorothy Menzel, the lines are associated with Nazca pottery between phases 2 and 8, but especially between 3

Geoglyph at Nazca called 'the Monkey'.

and 7, meaning that they correspond to all styles. There are tracks traced in the form of trapezes, spirals, or simply as lines that can attain kilometres in length. One also finds figures of fish, whales, birds, monkeys, spiders, quadrupeds, and even human beings. The most extensive studies are those of Maria Reiche, who made detailed observations of the technique of tracing lines and of their probable meaning. She thinks that most figures and tracks are linked to astronomy, for the purposes of agriculture, and it would seem that she is correct. Of course, she does not claim that all these tracings were instruments for measuring the movement of the stars, the sun and the moon, but Gerald Hawkins himself and other specialists have had to agree that many tracings permitted observations of the solstices and other astronomical phenomena.

Maria Reiche believes not only that the figures represent constellations, but also that they were most certainly places for propitiatory rites and festivals linked to production and to the cult. It is worth noting that all the figures comprise a kind of entrance: the spider through one of its legs, the bird through its beak, the monkey under the tail, and so on: these entrances are joined to vast, conventionally shaped plazas, which may also have an astrological explanation.

The fact that Gerald Hawkins, a specialist in ancient astronomy, did not find a correlation between all the lines and points where heavenly bodies fall or appear in no way weakens Maria Reiche's theory, which remains the most coherent of all those available today. Although she recognizes that the initial idea came from Paul Kosok, her specific

Lines and styled drawings of pampas of Nazca

The geometric lines and expressive drawings of the pampas in Nazca, are the admiration of scientists and archeologists, and still remain a mystery. There are several hypotheses about their meaning but no conclusions have been reached. There are some speculations that they might be a lunar calendar, an astronomic observatory, or just totems.

Doctor Maria Reiche has been totally devoted to the study of these lines for over thirty years and her findings might be considered of paramount importance among the studies done on this subject.

Researchers engaged in solving the mystery of the lines, have only pointed out possibilities which cannot be considered fully reliable.

Dr. Maria Reiche's resolute determination, unyielding utterly and sacrifice towards the success of her quest, have earned her the admiration and gratefulness of Peru.

contribution was to have observed that the establishment of this tracing system was in fact very simple and fully corresponded to the technical and scientific possibilities of the period.

One can therefore say that the great pampas of Nazca were both a kind of immense ceremonial centre and an oratory for the priests who lived in the nearby town of Cahuachi.

Danièle Lavallée and
Luis G. Lumbreras
Les Andes, de la Préhistoire aux Incas,
1985

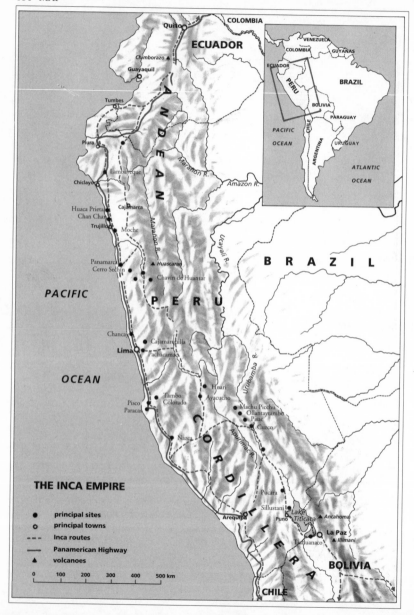

COLOMBIA

Quito

ECUADOR

Chimborazo ▲

Guayaquil

VENEZUELA

COLOMBIA GUYANAS

ECUADOR

PERU

BRAZIL

BOLIVIA

PACIFIC PARAGUAY

OCEAN CHILE URUGUAY

ATLANTIC

ARGENTINA OCEAN

Tumbes

Piura

Lambayeque

Chiclayo

Huaca Prieta

Chan Chan

Trujillo

Moche

Cajamarca

Panamarca

Cerro Sechin

Chancay

Lima

Cajamarquilla

Pachacamac

Pisco

Paracas

Tambo Colorado

Nazca

Huari

Ayacucho

Machu Picchu

Ollantaytambo

Pisac

Cuzco

Huascaran ▲

Chavin de Huantar

Marañon R.

Amazon R.

Ucayali R.

Urubamba R.

Apurimac R.

BRAZIL

ANDEAN

PERU

CORDILLERA

PACIFIC

OCEAN

Pucara

Sillustani

Arequipa

Puno

Lake Titicaca

Ancahoma ▲

La Paz

Tiahuanaco

Illimani ▲

BOLIVIA

CHILE

THE INCA EMPIRE

● principal sites

○ principal towns

--- Inca routes

— Panamerican Highway

▲ volcanoes

0   100   200   300   400   500 km

FURTHER READING

Arriaga, Pablo José de, *The Extirpation of Idolatry in Peru*, 1968 (original 1621)

Bakewell, Peter, '"Pigmentocracy": Race, Colour and Status', in J.H. Elliott (ed.), *The Hispanic World*, 1991

Bernand, Carmen, *La Solitude des Renaissants*, 1985

Bingham, Hiram, *Lost City of the Incas: The Story of Machu Picchu and its Builders*, 1951

Cameron, Ian, *Kingdom of the Sun God: A History of the Andes and their People*, 1990

Cieza de León, Pedro, *Chronicle of Peru*, 1864 (original 1553)

Duviols, Pierre, *La Lutte contre les Religions Autochtones dans le Pérou Colonial*, 1971

Garcilaso de la Vega, Inca, *The Royal Commentaries of the Incas and General History of Peru*, 1869/1871 (original 1609)

Hemming, John, *The Conquest of the Incas*, 1983

Humboldt, Alexander von, *Personal Narrative of Travels to the Equinoctial Regions of the New Continent, 1797–1804*

Keatinge, Richard W. (ed.), *Peruvian Prehistory*, 1988

Kendall, Ann, *Everyday Life of the Incas,* 1989

Lavallée, Danièle and Luis G. Lumbreras, *Les Andes: de la Préhistoire aux Incas*, 1985

Lynch, J., *The Spanish American Revolutions: 1808–1826*, 1973

McNeill, William H., *Plagues and Peoples*, 1977

Métraux, Alfred, *The History of the Incas*, 1970

Molina, Christobal de, *The Fables and Rites of the Incas*, 1873 (original 1573)

Morris, Craig and Donald E. Thompson, *Huanuco Pampa: An Inca City and its Hinterland*, 1985

Moseley, Michael E., *The Incas and their Ancestors: The Archaeology of Peru*, 1992

Murra, John, *The Economic Organization of the Inca State*, 1980

Nash, Nathaniel C., 'Archaeologist Wants to Reconquer Shrine for Incas', *The New York Times*, 31 August 1993

Nicholson, I., *The Liberators*, 1969

Parsinnen, Märtti, *Tawantinsuyu: The Inca State and its Political Organization*, 1992

Pizarro, Pedro, *Relation of the Discovery and Conquest of the Kingdoms of Peru*, 1921 (original 1571)

Prescott, William H., *History of the Conquest of Peru*, 1847

Rowe, John H., 'Inca Culture at the Time of the Spanish Conquest', *Handbook of South American Indians*, 1946

Squier, E.G., *Peru: Incidents of Travel and Exploration in the Land of the Incas*, 1877

Wachtel, Nathan, *The Vision of the Vanquished*, 1977

Xeres, Francisco de, *The Conquest of Peru*, 1872 (original 1534)

Zuidema, Tom, *The Ceque System of Cuzco*, 1964

LIST OF ILLUSTRATIONS

The following abbreviations have been used:
a above; *b* below; *l* left; *r* right; *c* centre; Bibl. Nac. Biblioteca Nacional, Madrid; BMNHN Bibliothèque du Muséum National d'Histoire Naturelle, Paris; BN Bibliothèque Nationale, Paris; MNM Musée du Nouveau Monde, La Rochelle.

CHAPTER 3

CHAPTER 4

Bibl. des Arts décoratifs, Paris
154 Drawing by Felipe Guamán Poma de Ayala
155 The temple of the Sun. Bibl. des Arts décoratifs, Paris
157 The Coricancha, surmounted by the Spanish church of Santo Domingo
158 'La *Chocolate*, native dance'. Engraving of about 1848. Bibl. des Arts décoratifs, Paris
159 Drawing by Felipe Guamán Poma de Ayala
161l, 161r Museo de América, Madrid
163 Drawing by Felipe Guamán Poma de Ayala
164 'Indian woman'. Engraving by Juan de la Cruz. Bibl. des Arts décoratifs, Paris
165 Drawing by Felipe Guamán Poma de Ayala
166 Illustration from Martínez Compañon, *Libro Trujillo del Perú*, 17th century. Biblioteca del Palacio Real, Madrid
168a Engraving by A.-C.-V. Desslines d'Orbigny. BMNHN
168b Chorillos man dressed for a festival. Engraving from Dupetit-Thouars, *Voyage autour du monde*, 1836–9. BMNHN

170 Drawing by Felipe Guamán Poma de Ayala
171 *Ibid.*
172 Portrait of E.G. Squier. Smithsonian Institution
173 Bridge over the Apurimac River. Engraving from E.G. Squier, *Peru: Incidents of Travel and Exploration in the Land of the Incas*, 1877
174 Machu Picchu: the temple of the three windows. Photograph from Hiram Bingham, *Report of the Peruvian Expedition*, 1912. BN
175 The road near Machu Picchu and the Urubamba river. *Ibid.*
176–7a Typical houses at Machu Picchu. *Ibid.*
176b First site map of Machu Picchu. *Ibid.*
178 Royal tomb, behind the temple of the Sun
180 Pottery drum. Musée de l'Homme, Paris
181, 182 Aerial views of the geoglyphs on the plains of Nazca
183 Plan and drawings of the Nazca geoglyphs
184 Map of the Inca empire by Patrick Mérienne
185 The inhabitants of Cuzco. Engraving from Castelnau, *Expédition dans les parties centrales de l'Amérique du Sud*, 1852. BMNHN

INDEX

ACKNOWLEDGMENTS

Grateful acknowledgment is made for permission to use material from the following works: (pp. 154–9) from 'Archaeologist Wants to Recover Shrine for Incas' by Nathaniel C. Nash, copyright ©1993 by The New York Times Company, reprinted by permission; (pp. 158–60) from *Plagues and Peoples* by William H. McNeill 1977, reproduced by permission of Basil Blackwell Ltd, Oxford.
Patrick Mérienne drew the map on p. 184.

PHOTO CREDITS

All rights reserved 16, 17a, 35a, 40, 41a, 41b, 55, 62l, 73, 78, 83a, 85l, 86, 97, 105, 129, 138, 145, 149, 154, 157, 159, 165, 166, 170, 171, 173. Artephot/Oronoz, Paris 18ar, 18b, 47a, 60, 63, 67, 78–9, 90, 93, 98–9, 100–1, 102–3, 109, 110–1, 132, 148. Artephot/Pestana, Paris front cover, 49r, Faillet 83b. Arxiu Mas, Barcelona 104–5. Bibliothèque d'Art et d'Archéologie, Paris 66a. Bibliothèque des Arts Décoratifs, Paris 155. Bibliothèque du Muséum d'Histoire Naturelle, Paris 13, 42–3, 43, 45a, 58a, 58b, 77a, 90–1, 94b, 107, 113, 130, 168a, 168b. Bibliothèque Nationale, Paris 28–9, 46, 48, 65, 80–1, 81. Hiram Bingham 114, 117, 122–3, 124l, 124r, 174, 175, 176a, 176b, 177. Bulloz, Paris 61, 64–5, 140, 153. Jean-Loup Charmet, Paris 26–7, 31, 59, 68–9, 108–9. Dagli-Orti, Paris 14, 27a, 27b, 32–3b, 35b, 44, 47b, 53, 74a, 74b, 74c, 76a, 86–7, 91, 94ar, 95, 96al, 96ar, 96b, 106, 116–7, 118–9, 128, 151, 158, 164, 185. Explorer/Archives, Paris 57. Explorer/Charmet, Paris 163. Explorer/Desjardins, Paris 21, 79, 88, 89. Explorer/Mary Evans, Paris 110. Explorer/Viard, Paris 112. Fiorepress, Turin 70. Gallimard, Paris 62r, 88–9, 150a, 150b. General Archives of the Indians, Seville 23, 131, 134, 136, 144. Giraudon, Paris 15, 19, 70–1, 76–7. Institut des hautes études d'Amérique latine, Paris 17br, 42, 45b. Kido 41r, 94al, 142, 180. Library of the Royal Palace, Madrid 66b. Mary Evans Picture Library 56–7. Loren McIntyre, New York 75, 82, 92. Tony Morrison, Suffolk 22–3. Musée de l'Homme, Paris 24–5, 29. Musée du Nouveau Monde, La Rochelle 12, 30, 36–7, 38–9, 48–9, 51, 84. Museo de América, Madrid 161, 162. Museo San Roque, Buenos Aires 72. Museum of Lima Front cover. Monique Piétri 60, 126. Silvester Rapho, Paris 32–3a, 68, 85r, Englebert-BS 126–7, Silvester 127. Roger-Viollet, Paris 20–1, 181, 182, 183. Royal Library, Copenhagen 54. Nick Saunders 123, 125, 178. Smithsonian Institution, National Anthropological Archives, Bureau of American Ethnology Collection 172. Jérôme De Staël, Paris 147.

Carmen Bernand
was born on 19 September 1939, and until the age of
twenty-five she lived in Argentina where she studied
anthropology at the University of Buenos Aires. Her
first fieldwork, carried out in Argentina and Peru, led
her to become interested in the Andean peoples. Later
settling in Paris, she wrote a thesis on ethnology under
the direction of Claude Lévi-Strauss, then undertook a
study of kinship and depictions of illness and
misfortune in the Ecuadorian Andes, which won her a
Doctorat d'Etat. She currently teaches at the
University of Paris-X.

© Gallimard 1988

English translation © Thames and Hudson Ltd,
London, and Harry N. Abrams, Inc., New York, 1994

Translated by Paul G. Bahn

British Library Cataloguing-in-Publication Data

A catalogue record for this book is available from the
British Library

ISBN 0–500–30040–2

Printed and bound in Italy
by Editoriale Libraria, Trieste